A JOURNEY OF THE HEART

A Father's Trip Across America With His Son

By Hugh Aaron

Published by Biblio Publishing
The Educational Publisher, Inc.
1313 Chesapeake Avenue
Columbus, Ohio 43212
www.BiblioPublishing.com
www.EduPublisher.com
www.stonespointbooks.com
ISBN: 978-1-62249-121-6
Library of Congress Control Number: 2013949263

Edited by Barbara Feller-Roth
Cover design by Ann Stein

This is a true story. To protect the privacy of the characters, their names
and occupations have been changed.

SECOND EDITION

Printed in the United States of America

ALSO BY HUGH AARON

Movie Reviews, Short Stories and Poems
My Life With Words

Essays
Business Not As Usual – Volume 1
Business Not As Usual – Volume 2
My Life With Words

Novels
When Wars Were Won
A Raging Flame

Short Story Collections
It's All Chaos
Stories from a Lifetime

A Letter Collection
Letters from the Good War

A Collection of Novellas
Quintet

A Child's Story
Suzy, Fair Suzy

For more books by Hugh Aaron, please visit
www.stonespointbooks.com

A BRIEF BIOGRAPHY

 Hugh Aaron, born and raised in Worcester, Massachusetts, was a Seabee in the South Pacific during World War II. After the war he graduated from the University of Chicago, where his professors encouraged him to pursue a literary career. Although he chose to make his living as CEO of his own manufacturing business, he continued to write. Only after he retired was his writing published. *The Wall Street Journal* also published eighteen of his articles on business management and one on World War II. He lives with his artist wife by the sea in mid-coast Maine, where he is currently writing plays.

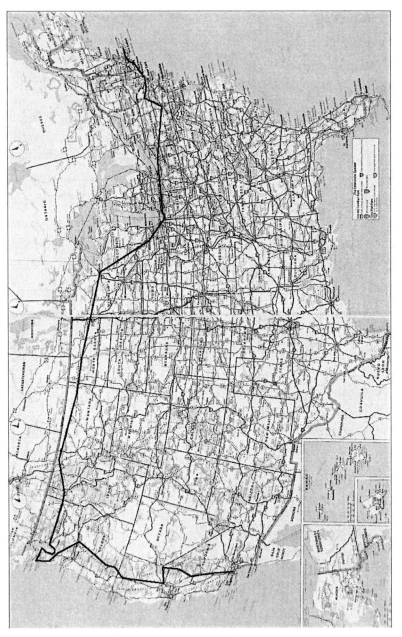

Harry & Danny's Route

CONTENTS

This book is dedicated to all fathers and sons who seek peace between themselves, and to all mothers who seek to understand the dynamic between their husbands and sons.

Hugh Aaron

There must always be a struggle between a father and son, while one aims at power and the other at independence.

Samuel Johnson

FOREWORD

When 60 year old Harry Simon decides to travel cross country by pickup truck with his 26 year old son Danny, he embarks on an odyssey worthy of the name. Homer wrote that it is a wise child who knows his own father; later Shakespeare countered with it's a wise father who knows his own child. This mutual wisdom both father and son put to the test as they take a journey that, at times, becomes as pleasant as going over Niagara Falls together in a barrel. Yet it also provides each of them with insights, motives, fears, failures and aspirations neither suspected in the other, much less experienced at close range.

In this blistering non-fiction account, Harry Simon and his son take the ride of their lives. It is a deeply moving, penetrating, and ultimately heartbreaking experience of two men trying to reconcile their differences in a love-hate relationship wrought from years of family turmoil.

Harry, a self-made success, is independent with a set of values. Danny, a freewheeling, indulged college drop-out, feels neglected, appears willful, caught in a downward emotional spiral, unsuccessful both in direction and motivation.

Though at times they hit it off, laughing together, agreeing on some points, mostly, however, the two behave toward each other as two masochists. Anglo-Saxonisms intrude occasionally and the dialogue is broken-glass sharp. It is as harsh as it is relentless with poignantly humorous ripostes to ease the tension.

Harry is searching his very soul to find harmony within himself and by extension in his life. Since "Diseases desperate grown/By desperate appliance are relieved/or not at all," Harry accepts Danny's invitation to travel across the United States, hoping to mend their growing alienation. Their constant arguing over decorum, driving habits, schedules, and what else reflects the adage that even kings, who command armies, cannot get their children to come down to breakfast on time.

Hugh Aaron makes the narrative gleam with some of the best prose written today—adroit, resonant, lyrical—describing America's natural wonders. Poetic images of forests, canyons, fields, compressed to virile discourse impress the reader with the beauty of creation as well as the human hand that is forever hell-bent on marring it.

Leo Rosten once quoted a Hebrew proverb: "When a father helps his son, they both laugh; when, however, a son helps his father, both cry." Danny, in helping Harry see their respective lives in their interaction, makes of that Hebrew author a prophet. Since Harry is Jewish (the Holocaust never far from his thoughts), he cannot be unaware of Proverbs: "A wise son gladdens his father's heart." In today's pop-culture, bumper-sticker philosophy, however, Danny's karma runs over Harry's dogma.

If, as Harry believes, that we are placed on this earth to suffer, to love, and to grow, then Harry's trip with his son Danny proves more than compensatory.

A Journey of the Heart is a wonderful reading adventure that deserves a wide audience.

RAMON DE ROSAS

DAY ONE MINUS ONE
Cape Cod, Massachusetts

Danny is my twenty-six year old son, a student at the University of California at San Diego. That is, I thought he was a student. But last April—it's now June—with hardly more than a month to go to complete his final semester and graduate, he abandoned school in favor of a full time commitment to his erstwhile part-time carpentry business.

"You mean you've dropped out of school?" I said, incredulous when he phoned to give his mother and me the news.

"No, Dad," he explained calmly, "I haven't dropped out; I've just taken an incomplete."

"But why? You're so close to the end," I protested.

"I'll go back. Don't worry. I mean it. I'll go back." Despite the resolve in his voice, despite wanting to believe him, I couldn't buy his promise. It was an old story. How many young male college dropouts had I interviewed for jobs with my company? I couldn't begin to count them. Before they had begun their careers they already had a sense of failure about them. It was sad.

His mother reacted mostly with anger. "What a fool," she said.

Deeply disappointed, I suspected that he had bowed to the inevitable. "Was it your grades?" There was a pause. I continued. "How bad were they?"

"Maybe I haven't been studying. I guess I'll flunk a couple of courses. I've had it with school. For now."

His business turned him on, he said. School seemed unimportant, almost juvenile. He had rented space for a woodworking shop and hired a couple of young

1

carpenters—Mexicans. No, they probably weren't legals, he said, but they were good with their hands and learned fast and worked hard. He had enough business lined up to keep them busy for the next six months—more than $100,000 worth. He would be making kitchen and bathroom counters and cabinets for a large contractor. The way he had it figured, more than half his income would be profit.

"I've got a real low-overhead operation," he said, sounding like a seasoned entrepreneur.

The words were familiar. I often used them in my business. It was the very same rationale for thinking I could compete when taking on new products.

"By the way, would you lend me a thousand dollars until June 1? For workers' compensation insurance. I've tried three banks. They say I don't have enough collateral. On June 1 I'll pay you back. I promise."

Good old moneybags Dad. I said without hesitation, "Okay. For collateral I'll take your promise."

My name's Harold but everyone calls me Harry. I'm almost sixty-two, retired from the plastics molding business. We manufactured house wares: wastebaskets and food containers, that sort of thing. A little more than a year ago, after three years of hard trying, I sold the business to a large corporation for cash. Selling a profitable company is a cinch, but selling one for cash is something else again. That was my last great act.

I didn't have to sell. Actually business was never better when the deal went through; for the last five years our growth was strong and steady. Maybe it wasn't the same as those heady years in the early seventies when the industry reached its peak and you'd have to be downright stupid to fail. We grew fifty percent a year then.

But the company was, you might say, fine-tuned those last five years. We owed our success to an open management style, which shared the "spoils" through incentives. Superior performance was generously rewarded; seniority counted less. Everyone knew the bottom line. Business friends said I was out of my mind for being so open. When the Japanese visited us—and they came often under the pretext that they wished to buy when really they were only curious about how we did things—they were surprised. Not like closed, dictatorial American company, they said. Like Japanese company. How come?

The resemblance was only skin deep. I also shared ownership with all the employees, which isn't a particularly Japanese thing to do. When the company was sold, everyone made out quite handsomely. Now you might well ask, if things were going so well, why did I sell? Because I deemed it the best possible time. After twenty years of more frustration and struggle than joy and satisfaction, I began to have a sense of final victory. Down the years I had lost and won battles but at last I seemed to have won the war. Although I had a satisfying feeling of accomplishment, I also sensed that my limits had been reached. There was nothing more to offer. Perhaps such awareness is partly due to one's age, one's stage in life. Were I younger, I believe I might have surpassed myself. The best time to sell a commodity is at its high. The best time had come for the business and me to part and for both of us to move on to greater things.

How easy it would be to spend the rest of this book talking about the company. Not long ago nothing seemed more important than the business. But now the subject at hand, that of a father and son, is what matters most.

You might also ask why I didn't keep the business for Danny's sake. After all, isn't it natural that a father would wish his son to take over? For one thing, Danny wasn't interested. He was bent on an independent course, preferring to make it on his own. For another I had some reservations about how we'd get along. I was a "tough boss", and I confess I haven't been an easy father. Were we to clash, the strain was bound to spill over to the rest of the family—to my wife and Danny's two sisters.

Three summers ago Danny spent the season with us at our home on Cape Cod working as a carpenter. He had a natural talent with his hands, especially in fashioning wood. He was employed by a local home builder who had taught him the trade during eight previous summers. Indeed he had become a skilled finish carpenter and maker of cabinets by that ninth season.

In late May he had driven across the country from LA in his six-year-old Toyota Carolla (on which he had already logged more than 100,000 miles). He planned to drive back to LA in late August by way of Canada. Would I return with him?

The question was startling. I was flattered, yes, even honored by the invitation.

"I'm not sure I can take the time," I said, groping for an out. "As you know, I'm in the midst of trying to sell the business."

"I understand," he said, "but if you can...?"

"Sure, I suppose I would. But I'd like to think about it. Hell, why not? Sure, if I can, I'll go."

Why the hesitation? Here was a shining opportunity, perhaps my last, to get to know my son intimately. I assume he felt likewise about me. This would be his chance to show me his self-sufficiency, to show me how well he performed in his world. He was an experienced traveler, having crossed the country numerous times, and toured Israel and Egypt, and later Greece and northern Italy, on a bike. Postponing his sophomore year at college, he traveled alone or with people he met on the way, financing himself from savings earned from a job in the shipping department of a computer firm.

Since World War II, when I toured the Pacific theater at navy expense, I have traveled very little, mostly on business to spots in the Northeast or to major cities in the United States. At twenty-five, bitten by the travel bug, Danny had seen much more of the world than I. He seemed to be running away from us, the farther away the better. Or was it from himself? At his age I had fled to college in Chicago. Afterward I stopped running and got a job. Danny is still running. He spent last summer hitch-hiking around Japan.

Soon I was busy supporting a family and gradually constructing an affluent way of life (which astonished and frightened my Depression shocked parents). It was an era of enormous expectations: With hard work and sacrifice, the American dream was a real waking dream within reach. So I buried myself in the business and ignored the rest of the world. Like most of us, I chose to stay in one place, where I then built a fortress—my business—to protect myself against life's pain. But instead the fortress kept all the pain inside.

Rather than traipsing off to Europe or the Caribbean, as so many of our prospering friends were doing, I had a second home built, the one by the sea on Cape Cod in which we now live. At first we used it on weekends and during week-long vacations—the most time off at one stretch I was willing to take. After a few years the family spent the summer there while I commuted on weekends to Boston— 150 miles in heavy traffic to and from our private paradise.

The house and the sea brought me relief from the usual tensions of the business. Furthermore, I believed, like Thoreau, that everything that matters exists within a narrow orbit, that what we think and what our senses absorb from the microcosm around us is enough. Matisse's garden replicated the entire world. Although Emily Dickinson rarely left her home, her mind was more alive than the minds of most of the worldly people who visited her. Our home on Cape Cod was all I needed. Not so my wife Jane, but that's another matter. Crossing America, seeing the sights, I thought, would be an unnecessary experience. But I knew being with Danny was my duty, and I shouldn't duck it.

When I agreed to Danny's proposal, I was in serious negotiation for the sale of the business, but I expected to have the deal consummated by our departure date. The prospective buyer in his letter of intent had set July 31 for the final signing, giving him plenty of time, he assured me, in which to "put together a financing package from my bank."

It's a rare deal that goes smoothly. On July 31 the buyer asked for another week to "sew up the package."

"Bad time of the year, Harry," he explained. "Seems there's always some critical vice president or a member of the loan committee away on vacation. But I'm assured they'll all be back next week. It's in the bag; approval is only a formality."

"You know I have a deadline," I said. "I promised my son I'd make that cross country trip with him."

"You will, Harry. It's a great opportunity. You

should do it. Wish I could do something like that with my son. I promise you'll not disappoint him."

The bank's vice presidents and the members of the loan committee returned from their vacations, met, and did the impossible: They turned down the prospective buyer's application for a loan.

"I need more time Harry, couple more weeks. I'm trying another bank. Got a connection there. This one's sure to go through. One of their VPs was in my class at Yale."

"Christ," I said, "You know I promised my son."

"I know, I know. I feel like hell."

But I didn't. I felt a strange relief. When I broke the news to Danny, he was magnanimous.

"I understand, Dad," he said.

"It's too big a deal for me to miss," I asserted.

"I understand, Dad."

"This time I think he'll raise the money. One of the VPs at the bank was in his class at Yale."

"Sure. I understand."

"This could be the biggest deal of my life." I hadn't considered that my going with Danny may well have been the biggest deal in his young life.

Jane went in my place. I was surprised that she was even interested. All along, saying nothing, she was my understudy waiting patiently in the wings for me to bow out. They drove leisurely for ten days across Canada to Vancouver and down the West Coast. Every few days she called, excitement in her voice.

"You can't imagine how beautiful it is," she exclaimed.

"Any problems?" I asked, meaning, how were they getting along together.

"A few, but we worked them out."

"Like what?"

"Well..." she hesitated, undecided whether or not to go on. "He won't smoke pot anymore, at least while I'm around."

"Damn," I said.

"He's really capable, Harry. I'm very impressed."

"With or without pot?" I said.

Now, three summers later, Jane is still raving about the trip. I see it was a big deal in her life. "How many mothers get to make a journey like that with their sons?" she asks. No doubt there's a special, sacrosanct closeness between mothers and sons that no father can claim. And how many fathers receive such an invitation? How many fathers would jump at the chance? Most, I guess. I should have gone instead, especially when I suspected the deal wasn't going to happen. It seems class connections at Yale aren't especially dependable; again the buyer's financing fell apart. Anyway, assuming he wasn't a bag of wind and would succeed in raising the money, wouldn't he have waited for me to return from the trip? Hell, I waited for him.

The truth was, I was afraid. I was afraid Danny and I would collide, perhaps irretrievably. Both of us were driven, controlling personalities. Each of us was bound to insist on having things his own way without compromise. Such intense animosity might develop that I would be forced to abort the trip and fly home from the nearest big city. Our love and friendship would be strained forever. It was too risky. Were I willing to admit it, beneath it all, my feelings toward Danny were uneasy.

After Danny's call announcing that he was temporarily leaving school, we heard nothing from him for almost two months. He ignored our letters and we failed after several tries to reach him via the telephone on his dorm floor. During the first weeks of his silence his mother was frantic with worry, then after a time she became angry. Finally in mid-May he called to say he was coming home for a brief visit.

"This is surely a voice from the long lost past," I said sarcastically when I heard him on the line.

"What do you mean?" he asked cautiously.

"I mean where in hell have you been? Your mother and I have been beside ourselves with worry. Do you know how long.?"

"How long?"

"Two goddamn months."

"That long? Hmm." He seemed genuinely surprised.

In retrospect, after discovering what had happened to him during those two months of silence, I regret my harshness. I should have realized his silence signified trouble. I should have realized that he was unlike his sisters (one two years older, the other five years younger), who always called when they had problems. Their mother was always willing to listen to their tales of unhappiness with boyfriends or disillusionment with teachers or dejection whenever they felt down in an unloving world. And I was always willing to send them a few dollars to squander on themselves to ease their suffering.

But Danny withdraws, clams up, and struggles to pull himself from the mire without help. He's a man, cursed by a society that condemns him to loneliness, the loneliness of having to conquer the world all by himself. He must never show vulnerability. He must meet his parents' unspoken great expectations.

It had been two years since his last visit, two years since his transcontinental trip with his mother. This time he would be driving across in his Dodge Ram pickup truck, the one I helped him buy for his small contracting business. Since the truck body had a fiberglass cover, he would use the truck to sleep in. Would he be alone? We were concerned about that. Certainly not. A friend from Boston—yes, a girl with whom he shared an apartment while he was at Boston University—was flying out to LA so she could accompany him on the journey east. What about the return trip? Would I go with him this time? The business had been sold. I was retired now. I had no excuse. But I hadn't changed.

"Of course, I'll do it," I stammered, bracing myself.

"You'll love it, Dad. Just ask Ma." I was silent while thinking how different his mother and I were from each other. He laughed. "Are you afraid?"

"Yes, I think so," I admitted, determined to be honest and open.

"We're going to have differences, Dad, but you don't have to worry. I've crossed the country five times with all kinds of companions and we always got along."

"But none of them were your father," I said.

"Once a guy broke down and cried and refused to go any farther. We made it, ended up still friends."

"Break down? Not a chance, but I'm not sure we'll end up still friends."

"Of course we will, Dad. You'll see." He laughed again.

There was no getting out of it. Not if I was to keep his respect. For the past year and a half of retirement I had been free of cares. Suddenly I would be put to a test. Crossing America with Danny would be more than a land journey. It would also be a journey into myself, something I had avoided doing all my adult life. The time had come to face the somber music.

Hearing nothing from Danny during the next two weeks, Jane became apprehensive. Had he left San Diego or hadn't he? And if he had, why hadn't he notified us when he departed?

"You haven't heard from him because he's on the road," I said.

"Well, he could call from the road," she complained, imagining the unspoken worst—an auto accident, a kidnapping maybe by some crazed criminal like the ones dramatized on TV.

Such thoughts crossed my mind too. I shrugged them off; they were too absurd. Won't we ever stop worrying? He's an adult, proven capable on his own, having traveled more of the world than we. But Jane felt no peace. Over several days she called the pay phone on his dorm floor until someone finally answered, advising her that Danny had left a few days before with some girl from the East. Children grow up, they grow into full-fledged men and women, and we keep feeling responsible. We can't completely let go. Jane couldn't, nor could I, although I was less willing to show it. Then his call came.

"Where are you?" I asked.

"Colorado."

"Colorado? When did you leave San Diego?"

"About two weeks ago."

"And you've only gotten as far as Colorado?"

"I'm taking it easy, Dad. It's gorgeous out here."

"You could have let us know your plans, you know."

"I'm letting you know now."

Suddenly his words cooled off my annoyance. "I suppose you are." Why had I doubted him?

"I should get there the weekend of the 7th."

"Which day? Saturday or Sunday?"

"I don't know for sure."

"We'd like to make plans, you know."

"Either day. I can't say more."

Hearing his tone become brittle, I reneged. "We're looking forward to seeing you."

With sincerity in his voice, he responded, "I can hardly wait."

And neither could I. Although Jane and I had seen him a few times on visits to LA, it had been two years since we had been on home ground together. There was a difference. At home where everything is familiar and friendly, we could be more like the family we once were. Or the family I imagined we were.

On June 7th, a Saturday, he called to tell us he was in Boston, or rather Cambridge, where he would stay overnight at his companion's apartment and take off for Cape Cod late the next morning. I speculated on this. He and the girl had already spent three weeks together. What did another night matter? It was all so casual: A man and a woman meet like animals in the wild, copulate, then go on to the next empty affair. Was that the way he wanted it? What about myself at his age? The question hadn't occurred to me. The only difference between now and then is the openness.

Danny arrived on schedule in his bright red pickup

truck, the elaborate yellow stripes along its sides leading the eye to a graceful curving design etched on the hood. He found us sitting on the flagstone patio behind the house. He wore shorts and a T-shirt that bore the words "It's just another lousy day in paradise" across his chest. His tanned face was partially covered with a close-cropped curly brown beard. He looked lean, painfully so, and I could see Jane wince at her first sight of him. Although shorter than I, his slenderness made him appear taller. He and his mother raced to embrace each other as I hung back, then he broke free and hugged me.

"Dad, Dad," he said unable to find other words. Grinning broadly, I patted his back.

"Welcome home, son," I said. I could hear music, the first chords of somber music, vibrate through my mind.

His week at home passed swiftly and fairly smoothly, except for two minor altercations. The first occurred within the first hour of his arrival. He proudly showed Jane and me his Dodge pickup truck, which he had bought new about three months earlier, with my assistance. For the remainder of its cost he was obligated to pay $100 per month for the next three years. He had used most of his savings earned from carpentry commissions to have a fiberglass cover installed over the truck body. Sleek, horizontal, screen-covered windows extended along its sides. The cover served his purposes well, allowing him to keep his carpentry tools protected and locked, to carry construction materials in any weather, and as shelter to sleep under on camping trips without the bother of having to set up a tent. As he traveled east across the country, he was pleased at how convenient the cover made things. By simply pulling into any secluded spot off the road, he would spend the night, usually beside a stream, where he and his companion could bathe and brush their teeth and douse their faces.

"It's neat, Dad. I put this thick rug on the bottom so it won't be so hard to sleep on. I hope it'll be okay for you."

I assured him it would. After all, when I was in the army during WW II I slept on the hard ground plenty.

"But you were young then," Jane reminded me.

"I'm not that old, yet," I said.

"'Course you're not. Christ, Ma," Danny said.

Jane knew better. She had heard me complain often of stinging joints and aching muscles after a day of gardening or an hour of sailing. The truck body cover was too low to permit standing, requiring that I crouch or sit or kneel when not prone. My knee joints were bound to hurt. Although I try to keep in condition by walking miles and swimming laps in the health club pool, it's no longer sufficient. I am like a fragile child after each new or infrequently performed position. Such pains are an impolite reminder of my decline, of my mortality.

"Travel light," he urged. "Though it'll be late June, you'll still need a sweater for the mountains."

He lifted the truck hood so that we could share his appreciation of the gleaming three-liter silvery engine silently suffocating under a gaggle of intricate gadgetry.

I shook my head and asked rhetorically, "How do they jam so much power into so little space?"

"You bet it's got power. Four wheel drive too."

"Why four wheel drive?"

"It's great for sand or mud."

"Sand or mud?"

"Sure, I don't need roads."

Now why couldn't I understand? Why had I assumed

that wheels and roads go together and that feet are for traversing the rest of the continent? I thought it wiser to keep such questions to myself.

Opening the door on the driver's side, he invited me to sit behind the wheel, where I could admire the impressive bank of gauges and especially the stereo and tape deck.

"Best made," he asserted, reaching across me to flip on an ear bursting tape of rock music. "I had it installed later. You can take any classical tapes you want with us, Dad. I listen to classical too."

"You do?" I smiled, both pleased and skeptical.

"See." He rummaged through a carrying case behind the driver's seat and held up several tapes marked Mozart and Beethoven.

"I'm impressed. And I've got a surprise for you. I'm listening to some rock these days—Dire Straits, John Fogerty, James Taylor."

"You're kiddin'." He gazed at me as if I had just been reborn.

I studied the dash to familiarize myself with the various knobs and stalks, since I intended to help with the driving. The five-speed stick shift was slightly threatening. "My father had a three speed shift," I said. "Never dealt with one of these."

"It's a breeze, Dad," he said.

"Is this the air-conditioner lever?"

Momentarily there was a telling pause. "No, Dad, this truck doesn't have an air conditioner."

"What do you mean, no air conditioner? How could anyone in his right mind living in San Diego not have an air conditioner?"

"I expected to put it in later. Just like the radio, it's

cheaper when it's not factory installed."

"Then where is it?"

"Well... I got short on money," he stammered.

"Short on money? Why'n hell didn't you tell me? And you expect me to cross the country in this—this human oven!"

"It won't be so bad. You'll see."

"How do you figure that?"

"If it's hot we just travel at night. That's when it's cool. Furthermore we're going to spend most of our time in the mountains, where the temp's always comfortable."

"I'm not keen about night driving," I said, the steam inside me subsiding. I gradually realized he had been wisely frugal. "That settles it, we're taking the most northern route possible. Chances are it won't be quite so hot."

"Fine with me," said Danny, staring at his mother knowingly. He wasn't about to tell me how naive he thought I was. Three summers before when they crossed the Canadian plains in August, it was hot, hot, hot.

The issue of the air conditioner had deeper implications. It was a prelude to the many compromises I had to make on the journey after the easy life-style I had become accustomed to. It prompted memories of those simpler early days thirty years before when I was courting Jane in my new '53 Ford without an air conditioner, without even dreaming of having an air conditioner. Who north of the Mason-Dixon line would entertain having such a device? I was as proud of that steamy Ford as Danny was of his Ram.

So part of being happy is enjoying what one has and not coveting what one doesn't have. This was a new idea to me, or at least its conscious formulation was. Of course deep down where all truth lies it was old stuff. I was swimming in an ocean of civilized comfort, which clearly I took for granted. In the early days, what did I have except the Ford to lose? There was that glorious, immense, ever-looming future, an endless stretch of time that is now my past, no longer mysterious, far richer, far more complicated than any imagination could have conceived. If only I could leap across the past to where Danny is and I once was, wouldn't I find something enormous to watch?

DAY ONE
Southern New England & Eastern Pennsylvania

Having packed and loaded the pickup the night before, we awake to a tangy morning and wash—I nervously—and are ready to depart promptly at 7:00. The morning is crystalline. The sun sparkles amid the trembling pines. Jane takes our picture in the driveway as we sit in the truck cab. I haven't shaved for three days. I look and feel as blowsy as a Skid Row bum. Why am I leaving this paradise, this place of my heart? Through the trees I glimpse a billion diamonds vibrating in the cobalt ocean. For weeks the tourists have been streaming to this spot, avoiding Europe because of the terrorist scare. And these days, New England, having a renaissance, is the most prosperous place in the nation. A month earlier Jane and I spent a week sight-seeing in Paris courtesy of our youngest daughter, who was there studying on a college semester abroad. I simply don't need another trip; it's too soon, too long, and too demanding.

But Danny needs it. He has expectations. He would be my friend, my guide, and my protector as well as my son. He would get to know me as he never could while submerged between two sisters. As he never could while I gave most of my attention to my other family: my business. He is searching for a model, for someone to point him in the right direction. What was I like at his age? Being the "success" I was, what had I done at twenty-five that set me on my course, that produced such "wonderful" results? Just a clue is enough, some hint to steer by, for he knows and I know he is foundering. Browsing through my library he found a book that he began reading when he was with us three summers before. Entitled *The Seasons of a Man's Life*, it is a book he never forgot.

"Take it with you on the trip," I suggested.

"You don't mind?"

"I think you'll get more from that book than from me, Danny."

Why did I say that? What he wanted from me couldn't be found in books. Danny laughed, thinking I was joking.

On day one, June 20, our principal destination is Pleasantville, New York, where Danny's sister Evelyn is an editorial intern for the summer at Reader's Digest, that sedate behemoth of the magazine industry. When she had applied for her internship, she requested Reader's Digest because it was near Manhattan where she wanted to live to see what it was like. School in Boston and Paris and now New York—not bad for a twenty year old.

Although they corresponded from time to time and talked on the phone on special occasions, Danny and Evelyn haven't seen each other for more than two years. They were years of distinct change in Evelyn. She had metamorphosed from an insecure, confused, awkward teen into a mature, attractive, self-aware young woman who seemed to know exactly what she wanted to do: to be a magazine editor. At Danny's stage of life—the mid-twenties—the change is slower, and the seeming suddenness of her flowering surprises him. Yet beneath it all, despite their radically different personalities and stages in life, both suffer from low self-esteem. Evelyn is striving to overcome her interior pain by sheer will. Danny is still thrashing about searching for a way. Each is conscious of the other's suffering; it is their common denominator, the basis of a hidden bond between them, the more so on Evelyn's side. As so often happens, the sister adores her older brother, looks up to him as her protector. She would never forget the incident at school when, baited by two boys lured by her shyness, she was rescued by Danny who held each of them in a tight armlock and warned them to lay off or suffer the consequences of his further wrath.

The day before our departure, Evelyn suggested on the phone that we meet her around 2:00 p.m., her chosen lunch hour, at a particular entrance in the rear of the publisher's main building. "The Digest is in Chappaqua, not Pleasantville. That's only the post office address," she explained, and she gave detailed directions. She is good at getting around places. After hardly five months in Paris she knew the Metro system as well as any native and had guided us about the entire city with striking ease. No matter what arrondissement we visited she had already been there. Yet she failed to recognize how adaptable and adventuresome she really was.

Passing New Bedford, we have a panoramic view from the highway of a sea of three deckers and old-fashioned apartment buildings spread across a long, low hill that rises from a narrow harbor, its piers jammed with fishing boats. The place sparkles.

"The harbor's toxic," I say.

"Looks are deceiving, huh," Danny says.

In barely fifteen minutes Fall River appears; vast old textile mills border the highway, relics of a once throbbing economy, of an industry gone south where it sought reprieve from high taxes and high labor costs. Signs stretching across the old mills' faces advertise their conversion to retail bargain outlets or small manufacturing businesses. But neither New Bedford nor Fall River are dying anymore. All

New England is experiencing an economic renaissance due to lower taxes, a burgeoning high-tech industry, and a significant share of the nation's defense contracts.

Less than two hours after our departure from the Cape we are snappily cruising amid the heavy commuter traffic along I-95 through Providence. The city's East Side near downtown abounds with simple early American and hulky, ornate nineteenth century homes that surround Brown University. Farther east are the pretentious eclectic houses of the wealthy. But downtown itself, now significant only for its small colony of high-rise office buildings, is a day place, replaced long ago as a shopping mecca by the all-weather suburban malls. There are a few bright spots: an attractive canopied mini-mall, an old factory building converted into a pleasant arcade of tiny, spiffy retail shops, and many restaurants (where some of the best Italian food in the country is found) that serve business executives and office staffs. The fancy restaurants remain open for dinner but this is the only attraction that draws people to a city core that has lost most of its human interest. Providence, tolerant of a strong Mafia presence, lies on the path between two world-class cities, Boston and New York, seemingly undecided which to emulate.

As soon as we cross the bridge spanning the Connecticut River, an exit sign indicates Essex.

"Let's go to Essex," I announce without warning. "We've got plenty of time to make it to Chappaqua by 2:00 and you should see this place." But I speak up too late and we pass the exit. "Get off at the next exit and backtrack," I say. "Essex is a quaint gem, relaxed, very small, easy to visit, right on the river, with a small ship museum on a point looking over the water. You'll love it."

Danny is game. Any unplanned escapade delights him. On entering the town and gazing at the old homes set behind broad lawns, I reminisce on my first visit there almost four years earlier. With another couple, Jane and I had stayed at the Griswold Inn for an escape weekend. Jane had wandered among the small curio shops, her happiest pastime. I recall we bought a six-by-ten-inch oil painting of green cliffs by a gentle ocean, and two thick hand-woven cotton rugs for our bedroom. I remember sitting in a rocker on the inn porch watching people and talking about small things. I remember dining at the inn in a room whose walls of painted seascapes were in motion giving the impression that we were aboard a ship on a slowly billowing sea. I remember dining at the Copper Beech Inn in nearby Ivoryton and enjoying its superb French cuisine, but not its price. Inclined to simple food, I consider elegant dining the most overpriced activity in which western man indulges.

I thought Jane and I were content then. And I thought she thought so too. Trying now to recapture that happy November weekend, I know we are no longer happy with each other. Our marriage is straining. Or was it so even four years ago without my realizing it? I am suddenly aware that our little side trip contains an ulterior motive other than just to show Danny a nice spot. I dwell on nostalgia, longing for that weekend, wanting to reverse the present.

Only 11 o'clock and Danny is hungry. I remember a bakery, an informal place that besides making delicious bread and scrumptious pastry, also prepared mountainous sandwiches to take out. The last time I was there the four of us ate our sandwiches on the street while window-shopping.

"The girls are terrific in this town," says Danny who finds them the town's most attractive feature. "Uh, huh, very nice."

"Young women are nice everywhere," I say. "Part of being nice is being nice to look at."

"I think this town has prettier girls than other places," he says with finality.

Although I enjoy the sight of attractive women, mature as well as young, I couldn't share Danny's overwhelming interest. Young unattached men are constantly and helplessly gripped by powerful libidos. Mine, although hardly dormant, is, because of my age, more easily controlled. Learning long ago to curb my appetite for what I couldn't have, I also recognize as I have aged, that less and less in life is potentially available. Desire is a futile waste of psychic energy. I will have to give my son the news that despite having the same equipment, I am incapable of responding to his indiscriminate enthusiasm for the other sex.

The food aromas in the bakery whet my appetite; we eat sandwiches of thickly layered tuna salad on fresh dark rye as we sit on a stone wall by the sidewalk. Beyond the wall is a trim colonial house and a small lawn on which a well-groomed man is stripping an antique chair of layers of old paint.

"Beautiful old chair," I comment.

"Isn't it?" he replies proudly.

"My wife's a collector of antiques," I go on. "I see it needs recaning. She knows how to cane."

"Great workmanship," says Danny, admiring the details of the chair's mortised construction. The simple old chair briefly brings the stranger, Danny, and me together. We say good-bye and the man smiles.

"Nice town," says Danny as we amble on. He lights a

cigarette.

"You've taken up cigarettes?"

Although too young to remember, he knows that twenty years ago his mother and I were avid smokers.

"I'm really trying to quit," he says.

"Why in hell did you start?"

"I dunno. I was up to a pack a day, but I've cut back a lot."

"Well, I used to smoke two packs a day and I quit."

"I know."

"How do you know?"

"You told me once."

"I did?"

"So you must know how tough it is. As I say, I'm trying to quit."

"Dammit, Danny."

His smoking is a sign that he's under stress, but more disturbing, that he's uncaring of his health. He had always been extremely health conscious, hiking long distances, biking to exhaustion, lifting weights, proud of his endurance and burgeoning strength. While he puffs away, he seems a stranger. It's an act of self-destruction. He knows better. I feel an unforgiving sadness.

Continuing on I-95 the traffic is sparse and the countryside wooded. Then near New Haven the semis gather from nowhere and stampede by left and right. West of New Haven I suggest we turn off to join the parkways.

"Before the Interstate was built, we had only the parkways: the Wilbur Cross and the Merritt. Beauty is, no trucks are allowed on them."

Never having been on the parkways, Danny considers them a great discovery. And not having traveled them for years, I find them more attractive than ever. Their trees have grown large, with branches arching over the pavement to form a cool canopy, and the shrubs on the median overflow with white and pink blossoms that sway like dancers in the breezy wake of passing cars. We are pleased with ourselves. After the interstate, this is high delight.

Reader's Digest is, contrary to world opinion, in Chappaqua, as Evelyn warned, not Pleasantville. A rambling multistory red brick Georgian edifice with a restrained stark white entrance dominates the large, prim, quiet, park-like grounds. Several paved parking lots full of cars seem contrary, as does the uniformed security guard at the entrance. Two more guards in a ubiquitous security car roam the road complex around the building.

In accordance with Evelyn's instructions, we drive to the rear of the building. A guard seated behind a desk inside one of several entrances has no idea where to find Evelyn. Try the main entrance, he suggests, the Rotunda. At the Rotunda while waiting at a polished wooden desk for the receptionist to dispose of some visitors, I study an array of Impressionist oil paintings surrounding the palatial room. Each picture hangs in its own panel in what is truly a small museum of masterpieces. Fascinated I momentarily lose myself until the receptionist, addressing me, brings me back to reality. After I explain my mission, she locates Evelyn in a directory (of more than three thousand employees according to Evelyn) but no phone is listed, no desk is listed, no clue as to where she is assigned.

"She's my daughter, an editorial intern," I say proudly.

"Try the training department. As you leave here go left. It's the building at the extreme end of this one."

The training building is refreshing after the sweltering temperature outdoors. Danny, wearing his traditional tight red shorts and yellow T-shirt, appears incongruous in the carpeted, softly lighted, comfortably furnished reception room. But there is no receptionist at the large desk with a computer, its monitor exhibiting green columns of statistics. Down a corridor leading off the reception room, I peer into office after office seeking some sign of human life. Even hullooing produces no results. Has the place been abandoned due to some sudden emergency? Or is this siesta time, corporate style?

At the end of a hallway I hear people murmuring in quiet conversation in what I take to be a classroom.

"Can you help me? Do the editorial interns work in this building?"

Blank stares: an editorial intern? Obviously no one has ever heard of an editorial intern.

"Go to the Rotunda. They would know."

"I've been there. They don't know."

"Wait in the reception area; someone will come along." It is fifteen minutes beyond the time we were supposed to meet Evelyn.

At the reception area Danny is in discussion with two crisp middle-aged men in long-sleeved white shirts and ties. Wanting to please, they embark on the search with deep seriousness. One observes Danny's decidedly informal dress with disdain, the other sits at the computer. After retrieving a directory on the monitor, he makes a series of phone calls and locates Evelyn.

"Thanks for your trouble," I say.

"Glad I could help," he says triumphantly. I suspect this is his most significant task of the day. The other white-collared man appears quite as proud. To the Rotunda again; Evelyn will meet us outside.

Emerging from the entrance, she is radiant at seeing us. How bright and fresh she looks in a long light skirt and stylish blouse. Her face, framed in brown curls (that she used to try to straighten), is smiling, flushed with excitement as she embraces Danny. Sister and brother, how they contrast, the properly dressed competent city girl now, and the young man looking like a slob, but unbothered. Standing by the pickup, I watch their joy, then she runs to me and we hug too. I had forgotten, my daughter is no longer a child.

"You two ride in the cab. I'll get in the back," I say.

As they talk nonstop on the drive to nearby Mount Kisco for lunch, I rock with the baggage in the rear. We park in the lot adjoining the commuter train station and choose a kosher delicatessen across the street.

Danny orders a corned beef sandwich, Evelyn her customary nude hotdog (for years she held to a diet of pizza, undressed salads, and meats heavily endowed with sodium nitrite) and I my customary cholesterol-free toasted tuna salad sandwich.

"To drink?" the waitress asks.

"No, to eat," I reply. "I chew my tuna."

Danny and Evelyn stop in mid-conversation to more fully grasp the absurdity of my repartee with the waitress.

"I mean, what do you want to drink?" the waitress asks amused.

Danny and Evelyn giggle. My joke is a hit, giving us an excuse to laugh, to show our pleasure at being together in this too brief hour and a half. It's all that Danny has given

Evelyn of himself in almost three years. I don't want their time together to end so quickly and I am already sad at having to leave Evelyn behind.

"It's not very much time," Evelyn says. Not knowing what else to say, they grow silent because there is too much to say.

Arriving back at the entrance to the Rotunda, we take pictures in pairs. A silver haired man in a business suit offers to take a shot of the three of us together. The stranger is giving me a treasure. I hug Evelyn good-bye; Danny walks her to the entrance and they hug and kiss. As he walks to the pickup, a uniformed guard beyond my earshot speaks to him.

"What did he say?" I ask Danny.

"Do you belong here?"

"Well, I suppose you're out of uniform."

"I said, no, do you?"

"Hey that's terrific," I say, admiringly. "This is a stuffy place. What are they afraid of?"

He waves to the guard who waves back.

Off we go toward the great open West, to the wide prairies, the huge mountains, the magical modern cities. Eager and full of a sense of adventure, we stop by the side of the road to plan our immediate itinerary. A teenage lad on a bicycle stops beside us and stares.

"Can I help you," he asks.

"No thanks," we say.

"Gee, all the way from California," he says, observing our number plate.

"Yup, and that's where we're headed," Danny says.

"Gee," says the lad.

"Gee," I mutter to myself, equally impressed by the

enormity of our journey.

Pennsylvania is next, a last-minute decision. I had planned on green, undulating New York State. One of Danny's rules is that tolls must be avoided. Forget New York State and its "rip-off" Thruway, he proclaims. Instead we cross the Hudson via the Bear King Mountain suspension bridge, a graceful span that connects low, steep, wooded hills on both sides of the river. On the west bank the deciduous forested hillsides are splattered brown due to gypsy moth caterpillar defoliation, the early summer scourge of Northeast greenery.

Danny has said he wants to know me better. Yes, I must open up. But we are generations apart. How can I help close the void that seems to exist between us? Will revealing my little secrets win his confidence and encourage him to level with me? I grope for a way to begin. Perhaps it's time for a little personal history. I tell Danny what his mother's and my life was like before he arrived, of my early struggle to make a living, of job stagnation leading to constant job changing. Unable to support a wife, who, teaching school, often supported me, I felt fragile and incompetent. The search for success was on my mind day and night. It was my holy grail, my fetish. My god those were terrifying years. Adoring his mother, feeling a failure, I once told her I didn't deserve her and she'd be better off leaving me.

Danny talks about his experiences with young women, of how he finds them cold, unfeeling, without a sign of affection.

"Why do you think they're like that?" I ask, suspecting he might expect too much of them, wanting their mothering and protectiveness. Maybe he comes on too fast, seeks immediate gratification? Or perhaps the modern woman is actually unsympathetic to the plight of the modern male, a creature burdened with the need to make good to confirm his manhood. Danny thinks the modern woman's coldness reflects the overwhelming character of our society.

We follow the Delaware River south on Route 209. Danny plays tapes of Cat Stevens, James Taylor, Bach, Beethoven, and Vivaldi. Although his musical taste is eclectic, he is forever surprised that his father, a product of the "super market music" generation, knows of Stevens and Taylor, and actually enjoys listening to rock music. I admit I've acquired an appreciation only during the past six months.

Seeing a sign denoting Dingman Falls, we detour a short distance to see the falls gushing over a cliff in the woods.

"Nice falls," he says. I agree, a very nice falls.

After a pleasing walk on a spongy, wooded footpath, we drive the narrow, tree-shaded road to the Delaware Water Gap, which had impressed me two years earlier when Jane and I had passed through. But this time it's a disappointment and I'm puzzled.

"It's okay, I suppose," Danny says without enthusiasm as we stop at a roadside viewing point.

"Yeah, just okay, I guess," I say.

"Wait 'til you see out west," he says. "The East can't compare."

Before dark we must find a place to stay the night. Danny has in mind to simply camp off the road near a brook or stream, but the prospect makes me uncomfortable.

"I'll need a john," I say.

"You can go in the woods," he says.

"I'd like a shower too. I'll feel better."

"We'll have the stream to wash in," he says. "It's lots of fun. Pam and I did it coming east. And look at the money we'll save."

"I don't care about the money, Danny."

We look up the nearest campground listed in Danny's KOA booklet, call ahead to reserve a place, and head for it.

"Pam and I had no sex," Danny says as we take off.

"It's none of my business, Danny."

"I know, Dad. I'm telling you for another reason. It's not that I didn't try. But she cried and said she couldn't. I felt sorry for her and just held her. She's troubled by something, I don't know what."

"It was very kind of you."

"I like her. If only she could loosen up, express herself. She doesn't react. When I'd point to a beautiful sight she would be unimpressed. Maybe an hour or two later she would say it was nice."

"We are so complex, Danny, so full of pain."

At 7:30 we pull into the KOA campground. Spotting the showers and the toilet, I am more at ease.

Locating our campsite for the night, we drive to a restaurant in Hazelton, a town in the heart of the hard coal district. Scores of empty stores and several buildings in varying stages of disintegration line the once prosperous Main Street. The city is dying. But many fine, old, well maintained homes, some veritable mansions, border the street out of the city.

"It's too bad," I say. Danny agrees. Why can't I

accept change gracefully even though it's such a fundamental ingredient of life? I see the loss of the past as wasteful.

On my first night to sleep in a bedroll in the rear of the truck, I'm apprehensive that I won't sleep well. Will I sleep at all? After I return from the washroom Danny disappears for a half hour. He is visiting our next-door neighbor, a woman with a motorcycle. He tells me later as we lie in the darkness that she is a waitress on her way from Boston to visit her parents in Virginia. This is one of her shorter trips; she has biked around the United States and even to Alaska. For the present she's without a job.

It's wondrous that a person can be so carefree, so unconcerned about the future. We talk of the necessity to plan for the future, to make reasonable forecasts. Until now, neither Danny nor I have mentioned his failed business. He suggests that its failure was due to poor planning. Minimize surprises; try to anticipate what will happen, I advise.

A few months ago the business had sunk like a lead weight in water, and Danny's morale had gone down with it. Without his parents' knowledge, he had holed up in his room for weeks, depressed and incommunicado, and had come home to lick his wounds. Had he also expected our journey together to be healing? I wondered.

A whippoorwill sounds periodically through the night. I hardly sleep.

DAY TWO
Pennsylvania, Ohio & Indiana

We awake early to a cool morning on the first day of summer, drive the pickup to the common bathroom near the entrance, and shower. Wearing only the previous day's T-shirt and trousers without underwear, I haven't experienced the natural chill of an outdoor morning since camping as a summer boys' camp counselor during college. But I'm reminded more of the mornings during World War II while in the Seabees in the southwest Pacific. The outdoors was our mansion then. For most of my life since, I've been accustomed to awakening to silent surroundings of walls with pictures and finely upholstered furniture and Oriental rugs. I have lost touch with the outdoors. The shower civilizes me once again.

We travel west on superhighway I-81 along the floor of wide lush valleys amid low green mountains. The road, narrowing to one lane, is under repair over long stretches. Danny talks of the effect of his parents' marital disharmony on himself and his sisters. His eldest sister seems to have maintained a healthy opinion of herself, but he and Evelyn suffer.

His eldest sister is recovering from a painful marital separation herself, I say, and is preoccupied with that. Or perhaps she has developed some immunity to the troubles of others, which seem minor by comparison to her own. Yes, I agree, her freshly won freedom has given her self-confidence.

Her husband, whom she had met in college, was a brilliant young lawyer with an assured future. She loved him unreservedly. However during their five years of marriage she found herself gradually suffocating. He allowed her no privacy, no freedom. He opened her mail, rifled through her pocketbook, investigated her clothing drawers, and allowed her only ten dollars a week for spending money (although she was employed and contributed to the household finances). If she spoke to another man he became insanely jealous. He constantly contradicted her in company and put her down.

They lived well on his large salary and bought a house, the house of her dreams. Finally she could take no more and left him. It took enormous courage. She forsook everything material she wished for just to be free of his shackles and become her true person. When her in-laws called bemoaning their separation, they asked that I intervene. I refused, saying it was best for both of them.

At lunch I call my friends, a married couple in their early sixties, near Chicago to confirm our impending arrival the next day. The carpet's out, they say. Listening to a Groucho Marx tape of his last appearance at Carnegie Hall, Danny splits his sides laughing. He has never heard the old comedians before. For the last ten minutes of the tape we hear another comedian run through his nightclub routine which includes the Sahara Forest joke, the one in which a half-pint sized woodcutter applying to a logging boss for a job offers testimony to his capability by professing to have worked in the Sahara Forest. "You mean the Sahara Desert," the boss protests. "Yeah, NOW" is the half-pint's reply. The new comedians don't measure up to the old ones, Danny says. True, I say, the new ones are funny but not fun. My son plays a Willie Nelson song that I like which pleases him.

"Know why I came home?" Danny asks, surprising me. "I need your love and Ma's. I need your reassurance, your approval. And I have a strong need to know you. To see what you're like."

I'm aware what I say and do are very important to Danny's future. Here at the beginning of our trip everything is going smoothly between us. We've had two cheerful, sunny, low-humidity days back to back. Will our journey end up as well?

In Pennsylvania, clover and mountain laurel are blooming in glamorous profusion. But along the Ohio Turnpike there is only monotonous flatness, greenery, and fields of low-growing corn: in other words, as Danny says, Dullsville. Oh, the McDonalds are impressive. An occasional oil derrick, bowing like a Japanese maiden, adds interest. The rivers are sluggish and muddy brown.

I need to bring up Danny's business debacle. "It's a simple matter of survival," I say. "Why did you risk all; why did you run yourself to the limit of your resources? And then what happened? Depression and withdrawal; goddamnit, Danny."

"I had to figure out what I was doing wrong," he pleads. "I believed I could rescue myself. I couldn't just quit."

I understand. It's hard to admit defeat. It's partly a matter of ego. I know the feeling. Knowing when to quit, to take a limited loss takes courage, perhaps more courage than sticking it out. Maybe Danny has learned that. Maybe his failure isn't such a bad thing after all. I let the matter drop.

Indiana is neater and more picturesque than Ohio. A distance back from the highway, comfortable, modern homes cling to small ponds, artificial patches of water in which tiny paddleboats nestle by short docks. This attempt at escape from environmental monotony seems pitiful to me, accustomed to the plentiful, glorious freshwater lakes of New England.

About 6:00 p.m. we pull into the small grassy field of a KOA campground in Middlebury, Indiana, a predominantly Amish community. A friendly young woman at the reception counter of the camp store recommends the good Amish food at the Country Kitchen. We are disheartened to find an enormous restaurant surrounded by scores of buses and hundreds of cars, a tourists' haven, not the place for two weary, sweaty, grimy travelers.

The air has become uncomfortably heavy with humidity. Remembering a pizza place, barely a shack, we had passed earlier, we stop for a delicious thin crust pizza. Gradually the clean, small shack fills with young Amish families. The women and young girls wear quaint bonnets; the men, dressed in black, have full black beards and black hair. Driving back to the campground, we pass more Amish people in black surreys with orange safety markers at the rear, pulled by handsome, well-groomed horses.

"How come the Amish eat at the pizza place and the tourists eat at the fancy Amish restaurant?" I ask.

"The local folk know the best places," Danny chuckles.

At the KOA, Danny takes a location not assigned to us against my protest, which I don't pursue in the interest of keeping the peace.

We have a hard night, especially Danny. The humidity is heavy on us. Mosquitoes and gnats attack Danny, the tenderer one. And I snore, adding to Danny's discomfort. At three a.m. I awake to the bleating of a train whistle and the distant rumbling of train wheels. I hear a clopping of horses hooves as an Amish buggy passes. This is a strange, lonely place and I'm happy to be with my son, who makes it less strange, less lonely.

DAY THREE

Chicago

Up at six, we discover a sodden, misty morning. A steamy shower in the messy, paper strewn head offers no relief, but in the cab we feel better on listening to a Fleetwood Mac tape while the sky turns blue. Our mood is further enlivened by a hearty breakfast of fried eggs and bacon in a busy restaurant with wide formica counters and large booths beside picture windows.

Again on the road we play John Fogerty, a Mozart trio, then a Mendelssohn trio. How good we feel, father and son, a harmonious unit, each so proud of the other. And the primness of the Indiana countryside, the wide cornfields and the warm air smelling sweet from freshly mown hay add to our good feelings. Small stands of trees, refreshment to our eyes, relieve the monotony of the flatness. For the next hours we hear a tape of Liona Boyd playing classical guitar, Bach, Albinoni, Vivaldi, the lilting melody of Greensleeves, then a Windham Hill recording. Danny and I, clearly lovers of music, a joyful common ground, are amazed and pleased with each other's eclectic taste.

In late morning the open, free countryside becomes the wretched cityscape of Hammond, Indiana, and Calumet City, Illinois. As a college student I visited the Calumet City strip joints, where I heard the rock beat years before it had captivated the next generation. The city's rutted streets, dotted with deep potholes, are empty because it's Sunday. We pass acres of silent steel mills and oil refineries and old, grimy, wood- frame houses.

"I used to date a girl who lived in one of these houses," I offer. "She was my forelady at the lampshade

41

factory I managed right after college. She was very intelligent, capable, conscientious and I liked her. Her immigrant parents were proud of her responsible position. They were kind to me. But I was afraid of our cultural differences and ended it."

Danny listens and makes no comment.

Was I wrong? Announcing her love, she gave herself to me on the bedbug-infested mattress in my southside apartment. Why, having long forgotten her, do I now feel sad? After all the years, I am unlocking old, repressed feelings of regret. Our souls are safe depositories of life's accumulated events and feelings, those we dared not express. Nothing is ever truly forgotten.

Traveling north through the streets of southeast Chicago, I search for familiar sights, but my memory is vague. We move through a neighborhood of wealthy homes where my very first love used to live. I can't identify the specific house, yet I know it's near.

"I wonder what's become of her," I say. "She was so beautiful. Her parents were Greek and rich. They objected that I was Jewish, and tried to buy me off, but instead drove us together. When her father died, so somehow did our love."

Why did I end it? I'm inscrutable to myself.

Danny seems to understand that I'm recounting emotionally packed experiences and really addressing myself. He simply listens.

Following my directions we drive to the University of Chicago campus. Indulging shamelessly in nostalgia, I show Danny my youthful haunts. But the old apartment building whose third-floor walk-up I shared with three other students has disappeared, and so has the very street it was on. It's now part of an athletic field. And where is Doctor Banner's old, narrow Victorian house and the garden I tended? An enormous hospital stands in it's place. I feel strangely betrayed.

"Things used to be better," I say. "The campus is too crowded, the new buildings too large, too modern. The human scale is lost. The place is going to hell."

So has a part of my past. Once I'm gone, after one generation, two at most, I won't matter. Yet my crazy ego wants to survive my body.

I may as well make use of the clean restroom in the new hospital building. I have to admire the stately granite edifice that replaces the old Stagg Field stands under which Enrico Fermi performed his monumental experiment. After all, what choice do I have but to accept the more crowded, riskier, decreased world I'm in? What's the use in resisting a relentless inevitability?

Danny reads the bronze plaque: "On December 2nd, 1942, man achieved here the first self-sustaining chain reaction and thereby initiated the controlled release of nuclear energy."

"And the uncontrolled release, too," I say. "The scourge or the savior of our time. I can't say which." Danny remains silent.

Heavy, dark gray clouds loom above, the air drips with humidity, thunder rumbles in the distance. We enter the majestic Rockefeller chapel, where I used to sit on occasion and listen to Bach on the organ. Nothing has changed here; the peaceful ambiance is the same. When the rain begins, soon becoming a torrent, we shelter ourselves in a doorway across from the old chancellor's home.

"This was an exciting place under Hutchins," I tell

Danny. "The college program was unique, experimental, designed to produce educated individuals in the old-fashioned sense. We complained that we were confused due to contradictions in the teachings; we felt lost in the absence of definitive answers. Our teachers smiled with pride. Our confusion, they said, was proof that we were indeed becoming educated, that we would have to decide what was 'true' for ourselves. We were taught to be responsible adults; no attendance was taken. Our grades were based on one six-hour exam at the end of the quarter in each course."

Danny shakes his head. "That would be torture for me."

"Sure, it was tough, especially if you weren't feeling well on exam day. Come to think of it, who did? Still, I thrived in this place, felt lucky to be here. Because I owe the university so much, I've made a contribution every year since I graduated, even when money was tight."

The shower is erratic. After running and whooping together through the raindrops to the pickup parked two blocks away, I'm winded. Our clothes are damp and cling to us. We cruise the remainder of the campus in the truck. As we pass Frank Lloyd Wright's famous Robie House, Danny studies it, mentioning that Wright was primarily a designer of private homes. Becoming an architect is one of Danny's ambitions, particularly a designer of private homes.

"The house doesn't seem as radical to me now as it did when I used to walk past it almost every day," I say. "At first I didn't like it, then it grew on me."

We drive across the Midway, the former site of the 1893 Columbian Exhibition, past an array of buildings new to me. Seeing 63rd Street is a shock. Gone are the old clanking elevated tracks which had given the street it's excitement. The deterioration, only spotty thirty years earlier, is now complete, creating a street of ruin. The old flower shop in which I worked is a ramshackle shell. Restaurants referred to in several of my short stories have been obliterated.

We recross the Midway to search for the apartment building at Kimbark and 57th in which I rented a room from the Kincaids for six dollars a week. They were a kind family, very polite and proper, with two college-age daughters. The Kincaids also rented rooms to two other students. Ever since, for thirty years, the three of us have kept in touch. One student, now an eminent biochemist at the University of California, married the Kincaid's elder daughter.

"It's Carl, Danny, whom we're going to visit in California. The other student became a psychiatrist practicing in the Chicago area."

The younger daughter, very beautiful, married a handicapped young man when she was twenty-one. Despite lifeless arms and almost useless legs, he became a Protestant minister. While pregnant, she was stricken with multiple sclerosis. Mrs. Kincaid asked me to give up my room for her daughter so that she could nurse her. The disease, moving quickly, incapacitated her, (she had become like her husband) eventually affected her mind, and killed her.

The face of the apartment building is clean, well maintained, in better shape than when I lived there, an anomaly in view of all else I've seen. No one occupying that apartment today could imagine the tragedy that had once occurred in their home.

Meandering through vaguely familiar streets, I point out the Mobil station on 53rd in which I pumped gas nights and weekends. Here is the setting of my early twenties. I started modestly, working for others, doing all sorts of jobs. It was years before I was ready to take on my own business. Danny started on his own before accumulating any experience or capital, before learning caution. Trying to emulate my success, he had skipped all the steps in between.

Although only 10:30 in the morning, we are hungry, for it's already been four hours since we had breakfast in the eastern time zone. At a crowded, sweltering restaurant near the lake end of 53rd, we find a vacant booth in an air-conditioned inner room. Apparently we've dropped in at a favorite neighborhood hangout. Everybody, mostly blacks and elderly whites, seems to know everybody else. They are loud and talk across tables to one another. I recall the race riots that took place not far from the campus across Cottage Grove and Washington Park. On the wrong street, a white man was in jeopardy.

"In the old days you'd never see a racial mixture this far east on 53rd," I say. "Progress, but not economic progress." The restaurant possesses a certain seediness.

Danny duplicates his earlier breakfast, as if he hasn't eaten for months. Perhaps the truth is he hasn't eaten well for months.

I wait in the restaurant men's room while a genial, middle-aged, neatly dressed, slim black man stands at the urinal and introduces himself.

"I'm Basil," he says, "from LA."

"I'm from Massachusetts."

"Hey, have a great visit," he says as he steps aside to wash his hands. "I hope you're having as much fun as I am."

A stranger brings cheer to a disillusioning morning.

Route 41, otherwise known as the Outer Drive,

hasn't changed in thirty-one years. I had driven it hundreds of time in my first car, a used '48 Chevy and later in my new '53 Ford. When I first came to Chicago, Lenny had often driven me down it to the Loop in his father's luxurious '47 Gray Cadillac.

Lenny was my first friend at the university. On most Saturday nights we took the Cadillac to the Loop for fried gulf shrimp dipped in hot sauce. I considered him incredibly wealthy, living in a luxury high rise in the east 70s, having his own room, a personal hi-fi and an enormous record collection. Handsome, smiling, and good natured with an ironic sense of humor, he drank too much. After a couple of years he confessed to being homosexual.

Voluntarily incarcerating himself in a mental hospital to be cured of alcoholism, he underwent an experimental gas inhalation treatment that would render him unconscious for moments at a time. "Cured," he married a strikingly beautiful girl and began drinking again. His drinking soon caused such a rift between us that we drifted apart forever. For years I have thought of him often, and now with my memory refreshed, I wonder how his life has gone. Perhaps I'm afraid to know.

Taking the Outer Drive along the lakefront through familiar territory to the Loop, so quiet this Sunday, we sail among the skyscrapers and down Michigan Avenue and Wacker and Randolph and on. Danny is impressed and so am I. The towers of the 1970s and 80s dwarf the once tall buildings of the 50s. My imagination is conditioned by what I once saw and knew. And now I ask: Where are the limits? Need they exist? For every gain, a loss; for every loss, a gain. Is bigness, tallness a gain at all?

Resuming our drive north, we pass the apartment

building on the near north side lakefront that my cousin Maxie once occupied. (It is also the scene of one of my short stories.) My cousin was a vociferous, beak-nosed man in his late fifties. A most striking ocean of metallic hair wreathed his massive head.

Deserted by his wife and daughter, he married a charming and beautiful twenty-five year old woman. He bragged that he was older than her father. On Sunday nights he often invited me to dinner at some of the city's finest restaurants. Living in the circumscribed world of a student on a tight budget, I felt like a guest in fantasyland. With his new young wife, he moved to Southern California to start over again, forsaking a big income from his well-established advertising business. Years later when I phoned him during a visit to LA, he refused to talk to me. I was hurt and puzzled. We were such good friends. The death of our friendship is an unsolved mystery.

In Evanston, we stop for a short while to view a Jewish Art Festival on the Northwestern campus. The air is hot, damp, and gusty. On to Wilmette and old friends, Jan and Ed Nast with whom we shall spend the night. Their small house is unchanged from my previous visit fifteen years before, except the children are grown and gone. They embrace us warmly. (How long has it been since we were last together? Thirteen years, back in 1973 on their visit to Cape Cod.) They are lean, trim, in good physical condition but looking far older than my last image of them. And what about myself? Have I aged as much as they? Are we mirrors of each other?

In the afternoon we revisit the art festival to see much that we missed, including paintings and metal jewelry exhibited in makeshift stalls. We watch a musical show on a small open-air stage and some dancers on the lawn. We listen to a rock band and meet crafts people the Nasts know. It is fascinating and fun although soon tiring in the heat. Being with old friends is comfortable and satisfying. Some friendships like some people endure and mellow. "It's good to be together again," we tell each other.

The Nasts take us to dinner at the Parthenon, a Greek restaurant in a rundown section on the western edge of Chicago's Loop. Rarely have I had Greek food. For Danny this is a first. Explaining the menu, Ed orders. The exotic dishes are delicious and Danny is a glutton. When Ed suggests seconds, Danny accepts and I am embarrassed.

After dinner we tour the Loop to view the gigantic skyscrapers that Ed and Jan identify for us. They deplore the crazily shaped, all glass city hall. Each building struggles for originality but most follow the simple, glass and steel Mies van der Rohe tradition. Entering the elephantine lobby of the Sears Tower while the Nasts wait in their car, Danny and I stare at an enormous Calder mobile. In the shadowed open spaces in front of many building entrances, we are surprised to find Miro and Picasso sculptures. We see many human touches in this otherwise overwhelming artificial forest. The impact on Danny is visible as his eyes gleam with pleasure.

"I could live here," he says. "I like Chicago."

"The winters are something else," I say.

"That doesn't bother me," he announces.

Ah, youth, I think to myself.

When we stop at a Jewel supermarket in a shopping center to buy ice cream, I am strangely homesick, yet I've been away from home only three days. Debarking forty-one years ago in Seattle after two years in the South Pacific, I crossed the continent to Boston, mostly by hired automobile.

It was the commercials on the car radio that gave me the strongest sense of being home in my own country. And now the mundane packages of familiar brands on the supermarket shelves have the same effect. In their ordinariness and universality they ridiculously symbolize our country's unity.

I phone Jane from the Nasts. She says she wishes she was with us.

"I'm certainly not having as good a time," she complains.

Months later on reading a few pages from a journal she had kept in my absence, I realized how lonely she was and how much she was hurting from our lost ability to talk to each other. She was hurting from our dying marriage.

That evening, sitting around a table eating ice cream, Ed and I talk of old times, of our brief careers at Jefferson Industries, then the world's largest lampshade manufacturer. Ed was resident psychologist and I a very young division manager. We were comrades in our outrage at the brutality of an organization blind to its employees' needs, with an eye only on profit. The president, an unpredictable alcoholic, was infamous for his frequent rages. It was us against him and his sick organization on which we nevertheless depended for a living. Neither Ed nor I stuck it out for long, I for only a year. But being victims of the terror made us friends for life.

Jan, taken with Danny, asks him of his plans and opinions. His replies are flippant. I'm dismayed that he doesn't take Jan's sincere interest in him seriously.

After watching the 10 o'clock news on TV, we lock up and go to bed. Danny and I each have a room. Our hosts couldn't be more gracious, couldn't make us feel more at home. And I sleep as if I were home in my own bed.

DAY FOUR
Wisconsin & Minnesota

At 6:30 Jan makes breakfast of fried eggs and cold cereal. By 7:10 we say good-bye in the driveway and Ed drives off in his new VW to his retirement-paced consulting work. Jan returns to her house to clean up after us.

Why is every parting sad? Because it is always a loss even if for only a few hours? Because from the moment of birth, from the beginning of our being, we need our mother and feel unprotected when she's not near? Because in only the briefest time the need to bond expresses and repeats itself? Yet I know that sadness at parting derives from the deep well of my soul. In only minutes on the expressway to Milwaukee I already miss the Nasts.

The southern Wisconsin countryside begins to resemble New England. No, its gentle hills are broader, its vistas more expansive. As in Indiana, houses huddle beside miniature ponds. The expressway takes us swiftly by Milwaukee, where it turns west. Soon we stop at a sign indicating a "Scenic View", a bell mound 1,154 feet above sea level overlooking the Black River Valley, fifty-five miles east of Eau Claire. After a steep climb, a prelude to more arduous climbs to come, we reach an open summit from which we scan the rolling countryside, scene of a great 1977 forest fire. In another direction are the rambling remnants of an exhausted iron range from which iron had been surface-mined long ago.

Madison is a homey city, site of the University of Wisconsin, an assortment of large nineteenth century and modern buildings crowded on narrow streets. The campus fronts on a lake. Small sailboats bounce in the wind at a marina. The imposing capitol building seems next to God on a height. Madison is a small, pleasing place for a drive around.

Parking the pickup, we walk through a cozy, tree-lined pedestrian street lined with shops. Danny lags behind to slow me down as I walk too fast. Throwing my hands up in resignation, I suggest he and I go it alone at our own paces. A strain suddenly and inexplicably develops between us. We are competing for control and go separate ways, but at the end of the street we come together. He is annoyed and hungry and we search for a breakfast place. Although he prefers not to patronize the local MacDonald's for his own unstated reasons, we finally settle on it. Grudgingly he orders his second large breakfast and I a sweet roll and coffee.

Soon the strain melts and we talk of his plans to attend an architectural school after he graduates from college next winter.

"Is that what you want?" I ask. "In view of your weakness in math?"

"If I'm motivated I can do it," he says dispassionately.

"Well, are you motivated?"

"It all depends. If I like what I'm doing, I'll be motivated. There's the design approach and the technical approach. I think design is for me. I'll have to see."

I'm disturbed by his seeming lack of conviction. And this leads me—or is it the reverse—to acknowledge my annoyance at his wiseacre, childish demeanor with our hosts in Chicago. Jan visibly cottoned to him. Knowing that, he played up to her. I am annoyed because he has placed himself in a financially dependent position while claiming to want independence. I am annoyed because he drives too fast and too close to the cars in front of him. He ignores the speed laws in high-density areas and near road crews. Although I have kept these thoughts to myself, my mood is turning hostile.

Soon after departing Madison we encounter a thirty-five mile detour along a two-lane secondary road through aquamarine crops of new grain and clipped fields dotted with neat spiral rolls of golden hay. Here and there we pass canopied cheese and strawberry stands. Stopping at one, learning that we have to pick our own fruit, we decide we don't have time because of the long drive remaining to Duluth, where we plan to spend the night.

I tell of my last trip across the continent with three other sailors and a soldier after returning home from the war. We had hired a driver in Seattle to take us across the mountains and plains to Chicago in his babied Roadmaster Buick. He wanted to lay over each night in a motel. Impatient to get home after being away for years, we refused to stop and took charge, taking turns driving through the night despite his protest.

We were veterans of a good war. I compare the hostility that greeted the Vietnam veterans with the gratitude, even adoration received by us after World War II: "Our war was fought by a unified country, for a clear and pure cause. The Japs attacked us and Hitler's ambition had no limits. But the war in Vietnam was always false. It was a setup by a persuasive, paranoid, egotistical president. And the innocent participants got blamed."

The road is two lanes through hilly, silent green countryside. Rarely do we meet another car. A series of cold fronts marches across our path as we move in and out of heavy thundershowers. We pass from bright blue sky to forbidding blackness roiling with anvil heads. It is frightening. Severe storm warning announcements cut in on the regular radio programs. They list the counties in imminent danger, including the one we are in. We listen to reports of tornadoes and golf-ball sized hail. But as the afternoon wears on and we move north, we are relieved to leave behind the area of most danger.

Duluth is a surprise. The city is strung on the side of a hilly range that rises steeply from the shore of Lake Superior. Its streets are thus arranged in a multilevel checkerboard pattern. Downtown is clean and prosperous, here and there restored flamboyant nineteenth century brick and granite buildings intermingling with simple modern brick and glass structures. A new massive convention center occupies part of the waterfront. An old restored ore carrier, a museum of the city's principal industry, rests alongside a new pier. On the summits of steep hillside streets, old homes look across the city to the lake. Most, needing fresh paint, are ornate, wood framed, steep gabled, of Victorian vintage—gross evidence of an earlier prosperity.

Deciding to take a more thorough look around in the morning, we follow Route 35 south, a curving expressway that winds through the green hillsides circling the rust colored lake. The road offers a wide view of the city, of the lake, and of the flat lowland that forms a large section of the shoreline. At the information center of a scenic overlook, a guide explains that two days earlier a violent storm that had also spawned tornadoes struck the area. By stirring up the lake bottom and increasing the flow of river silt entering the bay, the storm caused the lake, normally clean and clear, to turn murky red. The guide emphasized proudly that tailings from the iron mines are no longer dumped into the lake.

Thinking of turning in at a KOA, we consider the guide's suggestion to stay the night at the nearby Spirit Lake campground for a nominal cost. A preliminary inspection of the wooded summit pleases us, especially its isolation and lack of other campers. Returning to the highway, we have dinner at a nondescript restaurant nearby. The food is inauspicious, but our hunger is undiscriminating. As we talk, taut feelings uncoil.

"You plan too far ahead. You're taking over, making decisions without consulting me," Danny says.

"What do you mean?" I demand. "Didn't you invite me to choose the itinerary, which I'm doing quite adequately, I'd say."

"But you cover every detail, every possibility. I'd rather be more spontaneous. You've got everything figured out in advance."

"Well, all I'm doing is exploring alternatives. That way, there are no surprises."

We reach an impasse: Our personal ways are at odds.

"I'd like to drive across the plains at night," he announces. "They're dull. You'll miss nothing worthwhile."

"I don't think we should," I counter. "Furthermore I require a regular sleeping schedule. I insist on sticking to it."

He protests and I'm adamant.

Firmly I say: "Remember, I'm a paying guest (I had agreed at the outset to pick up the trip's entire tab: our food, gas and lodging.) so I have the right to choose our itinerary and set the conditions I need for my own comfort."

"You're not being fair," he says.

"Damnit, you should first learn to manage your money. Then you'd have some to pay your own way and have a say in how we do things."

My voice is rising. Danny's is icy and controlled.

"Why do you talk the way you do?"

"What do you mean?"

"Why don't you say what you mean?"

"I'm saying it."

"No, you always say 'why don't we do such and such?' when you really mean YOU want to do such and such."

"You're ridiculous, you're being overly sensitive," I counter. "You damn well know what I mean."

"Sure I do, but you aren't direct; you're manipulative."

"You're like your mother, trying to change me. Look, I'm sixty. This is me. Take me the way I am or forget me."

In a continuing litany I condemn him heatedly for his dastardly arrogance toward Jan, his gluttony at the Parthenon, and his boorish childishness. Now that we are sick of each other, I propose ending my trip then and there and taking a plane back home from Duluth unless he's willing to accept me and my conditions.

"Don't, Dad," he says. "Let's try to get along. I want to."

"Okay," I say, "so do I."

That night at the campground we sleep fitfully in our sleeping bags. The temperature has dropped to 40 degrees Fahrenheit, a shocking contrast to the humid 90-degree days we were used to. Having to urinate in the middle of the night, I don't have the will to drag myself naked to a nearby bathroom. Instead I stand shivering outside the pickup and aim into the dark woods. We are constantly awakened by mosquitoes whining in our ears.

While lying awake, I realize I'm disappointed in my son. I can't admire him. He used to smoke pot. Does he still? And now it's tobacco. He sneaks cigarettes when he thinks I don't notice. Damn, he knows what he's doing to himself. Why doesn't he wash his hands after going to the bathroom, the way he was taught as a child? He eats ravenously like an animal. When faced with failure he collapses. And although insisting on being independent, he doesn't look for a job but depends on me for support. Yes, my son is letting me down. Have I, his father, somehow caused this? How can I inspire him, give him faith in himself? I carry a vision of what I'd like him to be. Am I too critical and judgmental? But he's damaging himself and he's damaging me.

In the morning the unheated showers ensure consciousness. Our teeth may chatter, but water is water. We now agree on something: it's a night to forget.

DAY FIVE
Minnesota & North Dakota

Awake at 5:30 and on the road by 6:00, we don't revisit Duluth as planned but stop at a small breakfast place on the outskirts. Over a big breakfast of hot cakes, eggs and hot coffee, welcome warmth after our frigid shower, Danny revives last night's talk on planning.

"Sure I make long range plans," he says. "But on a day-to-day basis I live only for the moment, reacting to the stream of occurring events."

"I suppose that's what we all do," I concur. While I can't put my finger on it, we aren't in agreement.

Approaching Grand Rapids, Minnesota, an overcast sky turns to brilliant blue dotted with puffs of gray clouds. The temperature is in the mid-40s, the countryside flat, wild, densely wooded, all deciduous trees, many white birches. Barreling along at sixty-five miles an hour, we gradually outrun a long train of open bulk railcars clanking along a track that parallels the road.

Public radio's Morning Edition news program and British News entertain us for the next hour. Danny, listening attentively, is intellectually alive, interested in ideas, world events, and politics, and he enjoys good classical music. Yet he makes statements that strain credibility. For instance, he claims that often after a night's sleep he awakens five pounds lighter than he was when he went to bed. And he firmly believes that a particular inventor mentioned in Ayn Rand's *Atlas Shrugged* has discovered a way of creating energy from matter without any initial energy input.

"But that's against the second law of thermodynamics," I insist.

"This guy's gotten around it somehow."

"Well, if he did, he'd revolutionize the world; he'd be famous and fabulously wealthy." I censor voicing the thought that I think Danny's full of shit.

Danny states his disapproval of nuclear power. "Solar power is the solution," he says. "They should spend more money on solar research."

"Not a bad idea," I say, but I'm suspicious of his dogmatic opinionating. I have read of the possibility of safe nuclear plants and that nuclear waste disposal is feasible.

Grand Rapids, the first town of substance since Duluth, is prim and clean; its twenties-style large-windowed stores and public buildings appear well maintained. The newer plain, boxy, single-story structures are pleasingly designed and well built. We pass a large paper-making plant. But whoever heard of Grand Rapids, Minnesota? Isn't it in Michigan?

"Never knew there was a Grand Rapids anywhere else," I say. "Bet the residents here have to explain over and over: Yup, I'm from Grand Rapids. Nope, not Michigan, it's Minnesota. That's what I said, Minnesota. Well, you've heard of it now."

Midway across Minnesota on Route 2 lies Bemidji, a small, neat, clean city with a substantial new shopping center. Indeed all the towns in this state appear surprisingly prosperous and up-to-date. Stopping at a modern market, we buy fresh strawberries, peaches, oranges, and bananas. I insist we have fresh fruit and not resort to sweet, fat-laden restaurant fare. Since leaving Chicago, the farther west we travel, the more we are turned off by the declining quality of restaurant food.

And the farther west we travel, the more hauntingly

beautiful and stark the countryside becomes. West of Bemidji the densely wooded scape gives way to broad, flat, grassy expanses where cattle graze and grain crops are freshly sprouted from the dark earth. Here and there are large rock piles, old repositories from clearing the surrounding country. All the way to Cookston, some 114 miles, the highway is smooth, clear, double barreled. So broad is the land that even at sixty-five miles an hour we have a sense of creeping slowly down the road.

Danny and I make a breakthrough. He concedes that his perception of my "suggestions"—my ideas for our itinerary—as demands may be incorrect.

"Danny, I assure you they are truly suggestions, nothing more, and subject to your veto and further discussion."

The tension between us visibly eases. Touched, delighted with his new openness, I tell him of a similar problem I have with his mother: her defensiveness at my seeming attempt to control, her displeasure at my need to plan things in advance, and her frustration when I change plans. And I am more aware of her subtle attacks and put-downs than I let on.

"But maybe it's a matter of my perception after all and her hostility isn't real," I say.

"It's real, alright, Dad. I see her attacks too."

Are we joining forces against the common enemy: Ma? Is this the basis of our sudden rapport?

Cookston is a pleasing, lovely sight. Tall elms line streets with great old homes. A young friendly woman, plump, pretty, and blonde fills our gas tank.

"I'm a horse person," she says. "Ya like horses?" She quickly learns we are the wrong people to ask. "What kind of gas mileage you get on this thing? I've got a '74 Ford and it gets only five miles to a gallon—when I'm dragging a horse trailer, I mean. Where ya headed?"

"California."

"No kiddin'? Well, have a great trip, Okay?"

Pulling from the station, I say: "Cookston, nice place, nice people. Too bad we can't tarry for a while."

West of the town, the road forms a thin line across a land of immense farms. Great stretches of low-growing crops, broken by small copses of trees, roll off into the dreamy distance where land and sky join. A sign on a barn says Reindeer Farm and a big machine bails hay on the road's median strip.

The section we see of Grand Forks, North Dakota, is ideally designed to discourage tourists. Flat potato fields stretch away from the highway. Grain elevators compose a boring skyline. The road becomes a crass midway of restaurants, car dealers, and a confusion of commercial signs. Not a tree is in sight. North Dakota is simply tedium, both natural and man-made.

A lone seagull is flying overhead. "Thinks it's the ocean," I say.

"Must be twenty-six years old," Danny says. "All fucked up."

When I was in my twenties, was I confused? asks Danny. Did I have a direction? Did I know I wanted to be a writer?

"In a vague way I wanted to write as far back as high school," I reply, "and I took it half seriously after one of my college profs, a highly regarded former editor at *FORTUNE*, urged me to pursue a writing career. My first job from college was an entry-level position in the mail room of the

Chicago Sun-Times newspaper. Soon I moved up to the city room as copy boy, wrote weather reports, then obituaries, got to know the staff, the columnists, the managing editor. Although I loved it, I quit in less than a year for more money in industry. A big mistake. I should have followed my heart."

"But you finally made it, Dad."

"I suppose, looking back, I must have had the right stuff, the smarts, the drive, you know. Chances are I would have done well in most anything. But I took the hard road with no specific training. A degree in English is not very marketable. For years I moved from job to job constantly dissatisfied, frustrated, never feeling I was measuring up to my potential, not until I went into my own business at age forty-two. Then at sixty, dissatisfied again, I got tired and bored, and somehow disappointed."

"But why? I don't understand. You've realized the American Dream, something most men never achieve. I'm proud of you; you don't know how proud, Dad."

"Trouble is, Danny, I feel I've made no lasting contribution to the world. If I had become a writer I might have done it through art."

While I drive, Danny reads aloud portions of *Seasons of a Man's Life* by Daniel Levinson. Levinson writes that few men in their twenties feel they are getting anywhere. Few succeed at establishing themselves firmly in a permanent career. Few feel satisfied with their potential.

"Comforting to know you have lots of company, eh Danny?" I chuckle.

"Tell me," he asks, deeply serious, "why are you so impatient with my confusion and lack of direction when you were once that way yourself?"

"Because I forget and I want you to be spared my suffering."

"But don't you realize I can't be spared?"

"I know," I say contritely. "I'm learning and you're my teacher."

Maybe I disapprove of his pot smoking and maybe I'm dismayed by his aimlessness, but what must I do? Nothing, absolutely nothing, except to tell him that I'm behind him. But am I? Can I bring myself to tolerate his weaknesses? How very hard it is. Yet, at this moment we are learning from each other what is needed to foster mutual respect. As Levinson says, men in their twenties generally experience a crisis, just as I did and Danny is. "I also know you've had a crisis, Danny—two crises, in business and with a woman." I refer to his painful breakup with an intimate girlfriend of a couple of years.

"It was a lot like what you and Ma are going through."

"They say a man finds his mother again in the woman he chooses to love. You and I love the same woman not so differently. Hah! But when it goes wrong…"

"What happens?"

"I have a confession. I haven't always been faithful to your mother. I've had an affair."

Danny smiles cannily. "Yes, I know."

"You know? How do you know?"

"I've known for a long time. I don't know how I knew."

"My god! Didn't it bother you?"

"No, because I wasn't affected by it. My life went on just the same."

"Christ! Well, I had an altogether different kind of

relationship with her than with your mother. She was totally approving. We found nothing but contentment in each other. Still I never stopped loving your mother—but the two loves were different."

Danny nodded. "With her it was romantic and with Ma it's protective and caring, right?"

"Yeah, that's right," I say, startled by his insight. "We have room for loving many people, and can express all kinds of love. But some loves conflict, as with a wife and a mistress. One love can diminish another, though we may try to deny it."

"But you must have been unhappy with Ma to want someone else."

"Your mother's depressed, Danny, more now than ever before. I've been turned off. When I tell her I want to leave, she's incredulous, can't figure out why. Christ. She's pleading with me to stay, give it a year, give her therapy a chance."

"Will you?"

"I haven't decided. Of course you know I'm in therapy too."

In the middle of northern North Dakota, in the middle of gently undulating chartreuse fields, in the middle of beautiful starkness, we are in the middle of the continent. Rows of low silos line the road.

"It's a silo farm," Danny says. "Main crop grown here is silos."

Lost in myself, I wonder how our trip will end. Will Danny and I be friends? Will we find new respect and admiration for each other? Will the journey clarify or confuse our feelings? We are into a serious, most delicate business.

Nary a car appears on Route 2 on Tuesday in North Dakota. Under a blank blue sky in the prairie, pools of water appear inky black. A sign announces that we are passing by the geographic center of North America.

"Oh, what I'd give for a swim in the ocean right now," I say and we giggle.

Estimating our total travel time as two and a half weeks, with our fuel cost—five thousand miles at a dollar a gallon average—at $250, we realize how ludicrous we are since we can fly clear across the continent for $140 in five hours.

"Yes, but what a difference in the experience," I say.

"Amen," says Danny.

"Sure as hell, we're a lucky twosome."

The stunning simplicity of the prairie affects Danny. "It's really beautiful, not monotonous like the routes south of here or north in Canada," he says. "This is my seventh transcontinental crossing, and the most beautiful."

As we drive westward, a hot, dry southwest wind, like a mistral, sweeps across the prairie, bending the tall grass. The air has a sweet, subtle fragrance. For hour on hour railroad tracks run true beside the straight road. The plain, at first a calm land-sea, a vast tabletop to the horizon, becomes, hours later, undulating vistas, dunes of green and brown and occasional black water tarns with ducks floating among the bulrushes. Horses and cattle with calves feed on the high grass. Occasional oil pumps rear against the sky, curtsying like courtly dancers. It is an enormous, lonely, striking land.

Minot, North Dakota breaks the spell, as does the Ho

Hum Motel, "Where Comfort Is King."

"So what are the customers, Queens?" I say.

North Dakota constantly speaks with signs. "Enjoy North Dakota, Open Year Round." Sign on leaving Williston near the state line: "Stay in North Dakota, Montana Closed This Week." Sign at Gramma Sharon's restaurant in Williston, where I inadvertently leave behind my white sun hat: "We Reserve The Right To Refuse Service To Anyone—Thankyou." Sign on a bank marquee: "Whew It's Hot Out There—100 degrees F."

The towns we pass through are all the same: the same fast-food joints, the same midway strip of motels and gas stations and jungle of signs, the same monotonous, garish mediocrity.

In my journal (a bound notebook in which, while Danny drives and before retiring, I record in detail each day's events and my impressions) I write: "What a shame! America is fast losing its ethnicity. Forty years ago I noticed the trend; now it's a mass movement."

Many motel signs state the price for a single room below their name. The cheapest in Williston is $15.50. Weary and thirsty from the heat, we agree to take an air-conditioned motel room for the night. After all, the price is right. Cruising the midway, we choose the best among a wide choice of large and nondescript motels.

After cooling off in our room, we go to dinner close by at Gramma Sharon's, a large noisy room filled with townsfolk and truckers. Our dinner is uninspiring as we have come to expect of most dinners on the plains. Afterward, looking for the fabled Missouri River in the 100-degree heat, we drive through downtown on a wide, concrete main street of simple storefronts. Behind railroad tracks and an old bedraggled railroad station, we peek at a partially dry sandy riverbed in the distance.

"It isn't the Seine," I say, dashed.

"Can this be it?" Danny wonders.

"It was it," I reply. "It's gone temporarily into hiding."

Returning to the motel, we take cooling showers, lay at last in soft beds marvelously softer than the truck bottom and watch an old seventies movie, *The Blue Knight*, with Frank Kennedy. It seems dated, unsophisticated. At 10:30 p.m. it is still daylight. A thunderstorm awakens me for a short while in the night. The heat has broken, and so, I hope, has the barrier between my son and me.

DAY SIX

Montana

Montana, get ready, we're coming. West of Williston, the North Dakota land continues billowing, grassy, barren, and peaceful, incredibly enormous, lovely, and mysterious. As we enter the big M state, we find no sign to welcome us.

"Maybe North Dakota's telling the truth; Montana is actually closed," says Danny.

In eastern Montana, dunes of green and an endless expanse of crops flow to the sky, broken occasionally by a small colony of tall cylindrical grain elevators.

Danny says he isn't ready to return to school after he gets back to San Diego. We discuss his job-seeking plans. Of course, in the past he has been doing carpentry, working with his hands, but now he's considering sales, where there's more opportunity, he believes. After all, he's personable and communicates well.

"You'll make more money in sales, and can easily advance to a higher position," I counsel.

We review his financial requirements for the summer. He plans to find a job right away and become self-supporting, just as he always has every summer since he was sixteen.

At random locations along the highway we see crosses mounted on upright posts, which Danny explains mark the sites of auto fatalities. At Poplar we glimpse the Missouri, still low but more impressive than in Williston. Our pickup truck passes a car doing fifty on the endless road.

"The law is the law, but the land is the land," says Danny, doing sixty-five.

Entering Wolf Point we pass the Get & Go gas station, which also sells groceries, beer, and wine; we pass M & S Smoke Shack Mobile Homes; we pass the Tip Top Motel. Wolf Point is suddenly behind us. On our left we follow the Missouri, flowing scantily among the trees on a lowland that extends to high bluffs in the near distance. The two-lane highway is ruler straight. For half an hour a half-mile-long freight train rocks beside us in our direction across the grassland. To date we have seen only three trains, none of them long, none with a hundred cars, as Danny has seen on his more southerly trips. West of Glasgow the desolate grassland is immense under an immense sky. But three thin horizontal wire strands fencing in both sides of the two-lane road for miles tell us that the land, for all its endlessness, is tamed after all.

A mother duck and her babies parade in single file across the highway. Danny, traveling too fast to dodge them safely, passes over the babies as the mother scoots away. He is extremely upset until he sees in the rear view mirror that the babies are unharmed. Danny's sensitivity, his reverence for life, quietly affects me.

I recall our conversation at breakfast in which he spoke of disappointment with his native Japanese girlfriend, who would greet him coldly whenever he returned from a trip. Finding her unresponsive and blasé, yearning for a warm welcome, he would feel hurt. Strong feelings of emptiness and frustration are brewing in his soul.

We view the grain silos of Malta and the local Dairy Queen—ubiquitous in Montana—through a windshield etched with splatterbugs. Freight yards burgeoning with freight cars dominate the town. Corrugated metal Butler silos fill most of the remaining space.

One hundred sixty miles further on, we pull into Havre, the most substantial town on our itinerary through Montana. The quiet downtown streets are clean and well paved with curbs and sidewalks, the stores, neat and inviting. After a heavy lunch—too heavy it turns out—in a large empty Chinese restaurant, we need a good stretch and go for a walk in the bright, clear, hot air. At a small, pleasant, air-conditioned downtown mall, we buy soap and a plastic container for it. Farther on at a small, stately post office we stop to buy stamps. Spying a bookstore across the street I suggest we look for Norman Maclean's *A River Runs Through It*.

"It's a hard book to find back East," I tell Danny, "but they're bound to have it here in Montana, its locale. I'll buy it for you. You'll love it. On the surface it's about fishing and forestry, but on a deeper level it's about pure, unadulterated life, about love, hate, respect, pain, and fun."

"Norman Maclean," I explain, "is a retired professor of literature from the University of Chicago. He taught me Shakespeare back in '48. Although smooth in appearance, he was a tough, no-nonsense, little man. When I once complained of my difficulties with Hamlet, he suggested I spend my time finding answers for myself rather than whining and seeking ready-made ones. And it's obvious he made his point. I never forgot his advice."

The man who owns the bookstore says: *A River?* Sure do have it. It's a classic. Can't keep it in stock."

Written while in his seventies, this is Maclean's first published work. After the big presses turned him down, his own university press, unaccustomed to publishing popular material, accepted it and found a best-seller on their hands. He thumbs his nose at the big presses who are now after him. And I hear a movie is being made of his story.

At times my age weighs on me and I feel I'm too old to begin again. But at sixty, by comparison to Maclean, I'm still young. I may yet get published after all. His living example hits as hard as did his words thirty eight years earlier.

Shortly after departing Havre, Danny feels sick to his stomach and has to pull off the road. Professing puzzlement at his sudden discomfort, he squats on the road shoulder trying to vomit.

"You just ate too much," I say, agitated. "It's hot and the food was heavy. What do you expect?"

"That has nothing to do with it," he protests. "The Chinese food must have had something wrong with it."

"I ate the same stuff, Danny, and I feel fine." Convinced it's his gluttony again, I scowl.

Ignoring my diagnosis, bleary eyed, he asks me to drive and then clams up for an hour.

Now and then we meet a lone bicyclist traveling east. Bulging panniers hang over both wheels. Sometimes the cyclists ride in pairs, men or women, lightly dressed, white helmets strapped to their chins. A tandem passes, the man in the rear taking it easy while the woman in front is oblivious. Red faced, they usually appear to be suffering under the broiling sun.

"I pity them on those long uphill grades," I say, studying the low hills of the range.

"It's not as bad as you think. They aren't in a hurry; they take it a mile at a time," says Danny, speaking as a frequent long distance biker himself.

"What if it rains or they don't make a motel? There's absolutely nothing out here."

"Those panniers contain everything they need, their tents, food, rain gear. They're really having a great time, doing something important for themselves."

Danny's words helped me see the satisfaction they were gaining from what to them is a proud achievement. Again my son, my teacher.

In Shelby, a town of no distinction, the temperature has climbed to 88 degrees. I suggest we have the engine oil changed at a gas station after learning that Danny had neglected to have it done sooner because of his frugality. I pay for it and he thanks me twice.

On the western edge of town we catch our first glimpse of the Rockies, an uneven dark blue border on the horizon capped with faint white splotches. Fields of wheat continue to stretch away on both sides of the highway in a wide sweep.

At the motel this morning, I awoke with a severe headache that has lasted throughout the day, due, I suspect, to the excessive firmness of the pillow on which I slept.

"I have a neck problem," I inform Danny. "If I twist the wrong way or don't support my head correctly, I develop a headache. I've seen the X-rays. They show disc deterioration. I'm not the way I used to be, that's for sure."

"Gosh, you don't act like anything's wrong."

"Oh, I look healthy enough and I suppose for someone my age, I am. My lower back gives me trouble from time to time, and I get exhausted pretty quickly when I climb stairs or hike up hills. I've got trouble with my gut— awful gas pains. My enlarged prostate makes me urinate often because I can't completely empty my bladder."

"Gee, Dad, I couldn't tell. You seem fine on the trip."

"Well, I've learned to accommodate my limitations, live within them. We needn't really be concerned. But it's important to understand that I'm okay so long as we bear this in mind."

"Oh sure. No problem. I understand. Though you'd never know you had problems."

"As I say, I'm not the way I used to be. They're real, I assure you, Danny."

Freshly mown hay waiting to be gathered in the fields forms a graceful pattern of curving parallel lines. Approaching the outskirts of Cutbank, a wall of mountains, their summits streaked white, show in sharp relief off to our left. The radio from Cutbank announces a temperature of 86 degrees. The sight of distant snow is an anomaly, the sensation of its coldness hard to imagine. But our spirits lift as, weary from the heat, we know a cooler clime lies ahead.

After Cutbank the land is dead flat for forty-seven miles to the mountains which stretch across the land from end to end to our left and right. The misty blue slopes are now ribboned mostly white.

Again I recall my last trip across Montana as a sailor returning home from overseas. "You know, it's strange," I say, nonplused. "I don't remember the mountains. I must have been asleep or maybe it was night. Or I was so intent on getting home, I ignored them."

Danny is alert to every aspect of our surroundings. The mountains invigorate him, as the upthrusted peaks, their sides slashed by glaciers, lie silent and glorious in the afternoon light. Entering the range, the road curves beside a mountain wall of rock bursting a mile up into the cloudless blue.

A sign in Kremlin, Montana reads: "Where you're

only a stranger once." Waterton Glacier International Park, reputedly among the most beautiful national parks in the country, is one of the few Danny hasn't visited. After stopping at the visitor center in St. Mary to secure a detailed map of the park, we take the road into the mountains and follow the shore of a long brilliantly blue-green lake, to the Many Glacier campground. Danny's excitement is growing. While searching for a campsite Danny passes several that to me appear suitable.

"What's wrong with the ones we passed?" I ask, exasperated.

"Nothing, Dad, only I'd like to see what's available first."

"I think they were good enough. Dammit, we don't have to explore the whole campground, you know."

"Okay, okay, calm down, just calm down. Since I'm driving I think you ought to think of what I want once in awhile."

"And greed is man's undoing. You don't have to have the best. Whatever does the job is enough. Keep looking and you may never find anything as good as what you pass up."

Danny, silent, glances at me with disgust. Tired and hungry, I've become irascible.

Quietly I demand, "Find a place near a bathroom so I won't have far to walk in the middle of the night."

Immediately, thank heaven, the perfect spot turns up, making us both happy.

After setting up his small Sterno campstove, Danny heats two cans of chunky chicken vegetable soup, which we consume ravenously. For dessert we have raisins, nuts and chocolate mint cookies. Most assuredly it's a feast for princes. How refreshingly cool the mountain air is. A sweet, fragrant breeze hums through the pines and we feel at home.

Taking an evening walk into the woods before dark, we cross a bridge over a swift, clear stream. I plunge my hand into the water, which numbs it. The trail leads to a small crystalline lake, also bitter cold to the touch. On the way we meet a trim, gray haired lady from Cincinnati. She stopped at Many Glacier on her way to California to deliver her daughter's car. Wearing a string of small sleigh bells around her neck, she explains they warn the bears of her presence.

"Bears avoid people, unless extremely hungry," she says.

"But how do you know whether or not they're hungry?" I ask. "Seems to me you could also be informing them of where to find a tasty morsel." She shrugs, and laughs nervously.

"I saw a bighorn sheep in the high crags back there," she says, motioning up the path. "Been walking all afternoon. Really I went farther up the trail than I intended, but this place is so beautiful that I had to keep pressing on to see more. You know, at one spot I saw ten waterfalls all at once. I've visited forty-nine states; this is my fiftieth, and this is one of the most beautiful."

Inspired by her report, nothing now could hold us from taking to the trail the next morning.

As we sit in the woods that night near the pickup, Danny urges me to talk again of my youth, of when I was his age living in Chicago.

"What brought you to Chicago," he asks.

"Not what, but who," I reply. "After the war, I enrolled at Worcester Tech, a highly regarded small engineering school, but I dropped out in my first year. I hated its science-oriented curriculum, and yearned for a broader education. The dean tried to persuade me to stick it out, but I knew I was bound to fail. Several others were in the same boat, felt the same, including a close friend who transferred to Wesleyan and eventually became a professor of history at Northwestern.

"My road wasn't as direct as his. I spent that summer as a counselor in a Maine boys' camp, where another counselor, a forty-year-old teacher of social studies at the University of Chicago Laboratory School, (the elementary and high school that John Dewey founded and which the brilliant quiz kids of radio fame attended) befriended me. How often a mentor, some wise friend, changes the course of a young life."

"I wish I had one. I never have," Danny said sadly. "I never found anyone I admired who would take a real interest in me."

What about me? I thought. Can't a father fill that role? But obviously I hadn't. I continued without comment.

"Well, seeing my confusion, my lack of direction, he encouraged me to consider the University of Chicago, where, under Chancellor Robert Maynard Hutchins, exciting things in education were going on. No place could be finer if I wanted broad learning: courses in literature, the arts, philosophy, biological sciences, physics, math, economics, social science, and so on. As I mentioned before, Hutchins's aim was to produce the quintessential educated man in the old European tradition.

"And I believe he was right. Years later in business I found that many of my managers—science majors, some Ph.D.—weren't capable of making smart business decisions.

They didn't motivate the employees under them or deal intelligently with our customers. A few couldn't write a clear, concise letter.

"So I took the five hour entrance exam in Worcester, where a professor friend from Clark University served as proctor. By late September I still hadn't heard from the University of Chicago. Meanwhile through the good offices of a local rabbi who was a friend of the president of Roosevelt College (now university), a then newly founded school on Michigan Avenue on the fringe of downtown Chicago, I was accepted into the freshman class.

"Arriving in Chicago late September 1947, I immediately inquired at the University of Chicago about my status. Deluged with war veteran applicants eligible for a free education under the GI Bill, the University hadn't gotten around to evaluating my application; but promised to do so within two hours if I would return. The rest you know. I had to rush off to take twenty-two hours of placement exams, since the university's College didn't acknowledge courses taken elsewhere. I placed out of—was excused from taking— math and a foreign language, but in all other studies I had to begin at the beginning.

"Then I did something thoughtless, which still makes me wince with regret. Rather I didn't do something. The president of Roosevelt College contacted the rabbi in Worcester (my home town) to find out what had become of me. He was concerned that I may have had an accident. I never showed and hadn't informed him of my decision not to attend his school. In failing to do so, I showed no consideration for him nor gratitude toward the rabbi, my benefactor."

"I don't think it was so bad," Danny interrupted.

"I'm afraid I live by a strict moral code, Danny. I often find it hard to forgive my trespasses."

"Let me tell you about the school. The University of Chicago in those days was indeed exhilarating. In both lecture hall and classroom I had several Nobel prize winners, Enrico Fermi in elementary physics among them. The College, operating on the quarterly system, required that we take an exam in each course at the end of every quarter to give us a clue as to how well we were doing. But our actual grades were determined by taking one six-hour exam in each course at the end of the third quarter. Exam week was tough, but throughout most of the term we could relax and enjoy the process of learning without the distraction of grade pressure."

"You already told me that, Dad."

"I did? A true sign of age, huh. Well, early in that first year my forty year old teacher friend from the Lab School introduced me to a beautiful, brown-haired, brown-eyed Greek girl from his senior class who was infatuated with him. "Take her out, distract her, take her off my hands," he pleaded. She was an embarrassment to him.

I needed little persuasion. She aspired to become a concert pianist despite deformed thumbs, which resembled thin spindles. But her deformity was no handicap; indeed it may have been a motivating factor, for her playing was extraordinary. We soon fell in love, my first true love, much to the chagrin of her aging parents, who tried to buy me off. Eventually, threatening to withdraw their support for her piano studies, they forced her to transfer to Bennington College in Vermont. Our love, intensified by her parents' opposition, lingered for several years by correspondence and secret meetings, then faded after her father died and she returned to Chicago. Looking back, I know now I had a diamond, and lost it."

Throughout the telling of my story, I am reliving my early and mid-twenties, a time Danny wanted so much to learn about and which I see involved facing problems not much different from his. And now he sees. Therefore I must sympathize and not judge. I must remember where I came from.

Finally about 11 p.m. we are in darkness. An hour ago I phoned Jane and our words were warmer than when I called four nights ago from Wilmette. Yet the tone seemed strained.

"Do you miss me?" I asked.

"Sometimes yes, sometimes no," she answered. "Do you miss me?"

"I think of you often." Before hanging up I added, "I love you."

"And I love you."

Not sure why, I can't help feeling empty.

DAY SEVEN
Glacier National Park, Montana

By 6:00 a.m. I'm up and the only one awake in the campground, it appears. I learn, contrary to a preconceived notion, that campers are late sleepers. An escarpment that looms beside the campground is pastel pink and orange in the dawn sunlight. While I unpack the camera from its case to capture the colorful sight, two deer, one with small antler stubs, suddenly stand mute before me among the trees. Smiling, I talk to them softly as one approaches barely six feet away and stares at me quizzically. For a while they munch the carpet of soft green leaves on the forest floor then slowly depart. I have a ridiculous thought: There goes a happy couple.

Danny and I have breakfast in style at the Swift Current Inn located in the campground. I am as ravenous as he in consuming the orange juice, pancakes, bacon, sausage and coffee. Over breakfast, he tells of his dreams the night before. He is washing an elaborate automobile that he has retrieved from a lake into which it had sunk. Later he dreamt that he is playing with a parent bear and its cub. After trying to free-associate to the dreams, we both conclude that they are an attempt to resolve the conflicts in our relationship, that he wishes us to get along better. And to get on with his own independent life, I surmise.

Feeling happy with each another, we hit the trail to Red Rich Falls and to an indefinite point beyond in the Many Glacier area. A thirteen-mile hike, the trip is longer and more arduous than expected, with its steep switchbacks and narrow, frightening (to me) walkways along sheer cliffs. For the first time in my life I find myself fearing height, and I slog on prodded by the promise of exhilarating mountain views at every turn, of aquamarine lakes sequestered in the long valley below, of countless, silent, silvery waterfalls, of sun soaked snowfields on 10,000-foot heights. Each sight seems to surpass the one I just saw. The grandeur of it all overwhelms me.

On the trail we meet Jennie L., tall and trim in khaki shorts and short sleeve knit shirt, carrying a small backpack. She welcomes our company, voicing her preference not to be alone. Who in this isolated spot, she asks, would help her if she fell and hurt herself or were attacked by a bear?

"I know you two can be trusted. Two Jewish men."

"You are Jewish?" I say. She nods.

Jews have a sixth sense for each other, believe that other Jews can only be good, that there are no Jewish rapists or murderers or thieves. I ponder this delusion. Jews, even those who are assimilated into the national fabric, don't trust the rest of the world, not after Hitler, not after the world and its great idealistic democracies stood by, allowing the Holocaust. And the State of Israel, a political and military force to be reckoned with, is seen by most Jews as the ultimate security. Is this another delusion?

Jennie talks freely of her life, of her two sons in their twenties, of her unhappy marriage to an irascible, controlling man.

"But underneath he's really a kind and loving husband," she adds. "I couldn't abandon him at this stage of his life, now that he's retired. No, I could never hurt him like that. And I couldn't bear the loneliness. Anyway, we can't afford a separation. After dividing the money, we wouldn't have enough to live on."

When describing my own home situation, hers strikes

me as a mirror image. Annoyed with her incessant jabber, Danny disappears on the trail ahead. Hoping to understand her point of view, that of a wife, and gain further insight into my failing relationship with Jane, I'm fascinated with her story.

She complains of feeling trapped in the smog-bound, teeming, artificial welter of LA in which she was born and raised. She feels trapped in the anti-intellectual life-style of her husband, a former businessman, who can't abide classical music (he would turn it off while she was listening), who wasn't the least interested in art or literature or politics or ideas or life itself.

"His investments are his sole interest. We simply don't communicate. The pity is, I have the same problem with my two sons, who seem to be drifting."

"Your sons are normal," I say with authority. "They'll find their way, probably by the time they're thirty."

She admires Danny for his carpentry skills, for his travels far and wide in the Middle East, southern Europe, northern Africa, Japan, and around the United States. "He's got something better than a college education," she declares.

My marriage has become sexless, I say. Sex is gone from her marriage too. The opportunity for deeper fulfillment has grown impossible.

"After all, nobody's perfect, right? Most of my friends are unhappily married. I believe it would really be worse to split. So we make the best of a bad situation, don't we?"

So she spends the summer in Montana in the forest service writing brochures and in her spare time hiking the national park trails alone in the natural surroundings she has always loved.

Looking and acting a good decade younger than her

fifty-seven years, she ambles at a swift pace and frequently has to wait for me to catch up. We meet Danny sitting near a wide snowfield on a height just below the summit, which we decide not to attempt since we are growing tired and still have to make the trip back. The air is cool, gentle, and soft. During lunch we gaze between peaks at a series of cerulean lakes strung along a valley floor like a necklace of sapphires. Before lunch is done a wind is mounting and storm clouds are suddenly forming over distant summits.

On the way down I tell Jennie, "I think if we'd met thirty years ago you and I could have made it together."

"Probably so," she says grinning. "But I babble on so much, I'd bore you."

"The way I see it, since you can't talk to your husband, you talk to strangers."

"But we aren't strangers anymore, are we?"

In less than an hour, the constant action of slamming my feet onto the sloping loose stone-laden path to secure a foothold weakens my left knee joint. Only by keeping my leg stiffened can I avoid pain. The morning's glittering blue sky turns overcast, and the air cooler, breezier. Dragging behind, I worry that my knee will collapse altogether and I'll need to be carried. Knee trouble is new to me but so is the long physical stress. What other limitations due to aging will I discover when aggravated by tasks I have yet to perform? On reaching the campground several hours later, I'm no longer able to hide the excruciating pain.

Before parting Jennie and I swap addresses. I promise to call her husband when I arrive in LA. Sad that our hike together is over, that we probably will never see each other again, my heart goes with her.

Oh, what could be sweeter now than to stand under a

long hot shower. A sign in the supply store informs us that timed showers are indeed available for a dollar. We each enter a stall, strip as hastily as possible not to waste shower time, and commence lathering ourselves. My shower never turns warm and Danny's hardly develops more than a dribble. We give up angrily, unrefreshed, agreeing that we are victims of a great shower rip-off.

With plenty of daylight remaining, the weather increasingly foul, we decamp and drive along the two lengthy, pristine St. Mary's Lakes to the magnificent "Going To The Sun Road" across the waist of the park. Like gentle birds we cruise through the showery gray sky among thrusting mountain peaks and snowfields and waterfalls. Circling enormous gorges gouged out by glaciers, we stare into deep U-shaped valleys blanketed with pine stands and fields of varying hues of green. At the bottom of the gorges, silent swift streams appear as thin strands of blue. Such sights are unparalleled by any I have seen anywhere, neither in the mountains of my native New England nor in the Great Smokies, which Jane and I had visited the year before.

Early in the evening we make camp in a prohibited area of a crowded campground on the low, thickly forested western side of the park near Lake MacDonald. Weary from the long day's hike, we have dark beer and sandwiches at a park restaurant nearby. After we settle in for the night, a ranger in a cruiser stops at our site and politely asks us to move on. Grumbling, we cooperate. Some miles farther we enter a larger campground at the end of the lake and after much searching in the twilight find a site.

"What do you think of the trip so far," Danny inquires. "I mean, is it all that you expected?"

"It's wonderful, full of surprises—about you and

about myself. I'm overwhelmed by all the things we've seen. They're much more than I expected. How's it going for you?"

"I really didn't expect anything. I just wanted us to get to know each other better and I think we have. That's why I proposed our trip together in the first place."

Exhausted, he falls asleep before I talk again. Only 8:00 p.m.—the light remains until 10:30—strangely alert, I write notes about today's experiences. Why am I no longer tired from the rich, full day? Throughout the trip, by Danny's preference, he has done the lion's share of the driving, thus enabling me to keep my notebook up to the minute.

Since our clash in Duluth, I think our feelings toward each another have been steadily improving. These past few days have been completely void of friction. Have I at last found paternal happiness? Although Danny is noncommittal, I believe I'm fulfilling his expectations. And he is more than meeting mine.

Having seen so much of the park already, we decide against spending another day at Glacier. Tomorrow we plan to head for the North Cascades National Park, 450 miles due west. And by Saturday, the day after, we'll be dropping down to sea level near Seattle.

DAY EIGHT
Idaho & Washington State

Unlike all previous mornings, Danny slept until 6:45. He says he had a restless night, had a violent dream: A bomb dropped from a 747 onto a school full of students, blowing it up. He is shaken and I am concerned.

"Actually, I haven't slept well on the trip so far," he says. "I never had this trouble on the other trips. How are you doing?"

"Surprisingly well, better than expected. The bottom of your truck isn't exactly a waterbed, you know. But I sleep right through, don't even get up in the middle of the night to urinate."

West along Route 2 we pass through an unsightly midway, Kalispell, the first town of any consequence since leaving the park. Breakfast of pastry and coffee in a hole-in-the-wall is the worst to date.

"Ain't nutritious," I say. So we stop at a small supermarket and buy fruit for in-between snacks.

On the way to Libby the road takes us through Kootenai National Forest, which has been extensively damaged by fire. Entire hillsides are burned out, black, ugly, barren, like once beautiful women turned into hags.

"It's like a forest slum," Danny says aptly.

The stretch of highway near Libby is the poorest we've encountered thus far. It goes with the rest of the destruction. To our left is the towering, snow-patched Cabinet Range, weak replicas of the dramatic mountains we saw yesterday. Signs in Libby: "Thirty Is Not Old If You Are A Tree," "Happy Birthday Eleanor Langer," "Wreck Inn Yard," "JD's Zip-In Drive In."

I am constantly struck by the color of the rivers and lakes in these parts—a unique, undefinable, pale teal green, soft and cool. Since observing it first in the park, Danny and I have speculated on its cause. He theorizes it's due to the combination of water temperature and oxygen content. After mentioning it to Jennie, she claimed it was merely the reflection of the clean, clear sky. But last evening when it was cloudy, Lake MacDonald's pale green tint was as definite as ever.

"How about a little gunkholing for a change?" I suggest.

A small tangent off the highway takes us to Kootenai Falls on the full, briskly flowing Kootenai River which winds back and forth beside and beneath Route 2. Since the walking path to the falls follows a steep grade, I tell Danny to go alone while I remain in the small dirt parking area with the pickup. My knee, although improving, is still troublesome.

Resting by a rustic fence, I'm approached by elderly Don McGrady who introduces himself with a handshake and proffers a small book of ballads for my examination and perhaps purchase.

"I began writing these things in my early fifties," he reminisces. "Didn't know I had it in me. Yep, sold over thirty thousand copies so far. It hasn't made me rich, but it's something."

I tell him that I'm also "trying my hand at the craft," having already written a novel and several short stories and some children's poetry, all unpublished.

"There's a press in Chicago prints the stuff for me. Y'oughta contact them. Good quality, reasonable."

"What about marketing the material," I ask.

"Well, to tell the truth it takes lots of work. I've had to become what I never thought I'd be: a salesman. When I was younger and all full of vinegar I was a cowboy in Wyoming, an oil well hunky in the Dakotas, a farm hand in eastern Montana, anything you can name. The wife and me used to make trips all through the Southwest selling my ballads to the curio shops and small bookstores, and you know we never came back with less money than we left with."

After reading a small selection of his poetry and finding his writing warm and thoughtful, I buy one of his small paper-bound volumes for three dollars.

"Y'oughta see the falls," he advises.

"Can't, sore knee." I pat it gingerly.

"Oh, that's too bad."

"Course when you get to be seventy-two like me, you have those kind of problems, especially when you try to keep up with the young ones."

I gather that he assumes, correctly of course, that I'm no match for Danny. "I'm ten years younger than you," I reply, implying that I shouldn't be having such problems.

"That's when it happens. I remember I began having troubles around your age too. My advice: take it easy. Slow down and you'll have better years." Seeing me dutifully humbled, he goes on. "My wife is ailing now; we can't make those sales trips anymore so I come here to the falls to sell my poems. I do pretty good, under the circumstances."

When Danny returns I introduce him to the poet. Mr. McGrady takes the book from my hand and inscribes it simply: "To Harry and Danny" and the date. Not very imaginative, yet I am pleased.

On our way once again, past Troy we spot a bright

purple barn. Wow! Time for playing my two rock tapes, Dire Straits and Centerfield, which I donate to Danny, much to his pleasure.

"I think men my age have a particularly hard time in our society," he says out of the blue. "The root cause, I think, is the macho image we try to live by. It's in our movies, our advertising—you know the Marlboro Man—a kind of super he-man we all aspire to be. The image is right on the surface, immediate, without subtlety."

"Yeah, and you guys are under such pressure to be successful, too," I add. "To achieve some great materialistic goal while still young, actually because you're young, which of course is usually impossible to do."

"But young women aren't under such pressure," says Danny, "although nowadays they're striving to assume the male role in their struggle for equality."

"Right. They want to be both male and female and they want to be neither. So they're losing their identity as women. Take your mother. She no longer wishes to be a housewife, performing all the chores that befit that role. She tells me I must now fend for myself." The thought flits across my mind that Jennie, expressing the same wish, had gained my sympathy, my understanding. Why not my wife? But Danny and I are now on an anti-woman, anti-mother/wife roll. "And she's always preaching, telling me where I'm wrong."

"And how! To me, too, and the girls (his sisters). But I've learned how to turn it off. I just say, 'Right, Ma, You're right, Ma.'"

"Anyway," I join in, "what right does she have to preach to me? Does she have more experience or wisdom than I do? Not less maybe, I'll grant her, but certainly not more."

We play Dire Straits over again. A few months ago when Danny was feeling down I wrote him a letter in which I copied the heartfelt, comforting lyrics of "Why Worry" from that album.

"Why worry, there should be laughter after pain,
There should be sunshine after rain,
These things have always been the same,
So why worry now?"

How can I teach him to accept pain as the flip side of joy, the laughter that follows, the sunshine after rain? How can I teach myself to my core that this is so?

At the time he was surprised that I knew the song, indeed that I had any acquaintance at all with Mark Knopfler, its composer. He repeated his amazement.

"You've changed, Dad, You've opened up. You're looser than you used to be. I imagine along the way you must have admitted to yourself that you were wrong about some things."

"Well, don't you think I've admitted error from time to time on this trip?" I ask. "I'm beginning to discover the more I know, the less I know."

Basin and range, basin and range crossing Idaho. We travel the length of a basin to its terminus at Coeur d'Alene, a civilized town of busy streets and brick buildings wrapped around the mid-portion of a large lake, altitude 2,187 feet. Taking lunch at a citified restaurant that replicates the twenties style in the west, we perceive it erroneously as surely the most elegant we've ever had. Well, why not enjoy kidding ourselves once in a while? So our lifestyle is improving and we've come down more than 8,000 feet.

Entering Spokane via I-90, we see an enormous junkyard of neat, endless rows of car wrecks set up on blocks. There's an elaborate water slide and people in bathing suits walking up a concrete ramp for their next run down. Spokane—the biggest city since Chicago, 1,700 miles to the east. Spokane—entrance to the high, flat desert plateau of central Washington State in which great farms dare to thrive. Spokane—where in late June it is hot and humid, where we view a double rainbow high in the mackerel sky, where we zip past on an expressway similar to all other expressways and say: "Hello Spokane," "So that was Spokane," "Goodbye Spokane."

Danny complains that at night he can't sleep because of the biting insects—mosquitoes and whatever else—trapped in the truck with us. They don't bother me, I say, which gives him little comfort.

"You're an insect beacon like your mother; both of you are allergic. You know you've inherited a lot of her characteristics—her slender build; her inner silence, although you are getting noisier; her moral strength."

"I do feel beneath it all I am strong, Dad."

But he's such a slob, I think. In the cab behind our seats it's a helter-skelter of sweaters and shirts, camera, maps, food, what have you. I can never find things, but miraculously he does.

Nearby, dust devils swirl across the freshly furrowed bare earth.

The Grand Coulee Dam is set in a barren valley at the head of a wide blue lake, awesome in scale, one mile wide, largest concrete structure in the world, one of FDR's greatest achievements, completed during World War II in

1942. It is now fifty years old. Its most recent addition, constructed in the seventies generates three times the power of any earlier generating facility. After driving across the top of the dam, we don't take time to tour the new generating station, which is open to the public.

The twisting Columbia River slices deeply through the high desert. We cross it at Grand Coulee and later at Chief Joseph Dam. I phone for a reservation at a KOA in Winthrop above Twisp.

"Where everyone lisps, Danny. How can they do otherwise?"

Leaving Grand Coulee we drive under a spokelike network of thick, drooping power lines supported by giant steel towers marching off in all directions. They have a simple proud, artificial beauty. The road takes wide curves down into a broad, treeless chasm, then up to a new height and down again into another chasm. Everywhere is raw, rolling desert carpeted with pale green chaparral, forever the same, empty, lonely, soulless. A bittersweet, fresh fragrance is in the air. The Cascade Range appears off in the dust-laden haze.

Less than a half hour farther west, Chief Joseph Dam is a surprise. Tuning in our radio to the appropriate signal specified by a road sign, we learn that, when completed, Chief Joseph will produce more electricity than any other dam in the country; it will be one of the largest power plants in the world.

"Never heard of this place," I say. "How come nobody knows about it? How come a place this big and important remains a secret?" Danny shrugs, just as puzzled.

Crossing the Columbia past the dam, we pause at a park-like viewing area just abandoned by its other visitor, a camper. We study the harsh, neatly formed, fascinating panorama, the dam and the extensive lake behind it, in appreciative silence. Posters tell of the attempt to replace the original wildlife habitats with new man-made ones. They tell the sorry story of Chief Joseph and his people.

After battling the white man in Montana, where his tribe had been relocated, the chief surrendered upon being told that they could return to their home ground in Oregon. But it was a deception, and the chief and his people were instead sent to a reservation on this high, barren plateau in Washington.

I felt shame, perhaps the sort of shame that recent generations of Germans must feel towards their forefathers' crimes against the Jews.

"Dammit. The least we could do for Chief Joseph was to name one of the world's largest dams after him. Too late maybe, but it's something after all, isn't it?" Yes, Danny nods.

On the road to Okanogan, U.S. 97, we wend our way through an extended garden along the Salmon River. On the river side to our left flourishes a verdant paradise of green crops, fruit trees, and tall hardwoods, to our right open sterile desert with blowing chapparal. The contrast is startling.

From the Dakotas to mid-Washington State, irrigation abounds; it is the common motif. Everywhere shooting plumes of water cover and soak the land in the heat of the afternoon. This day it must be in the 90s, and dry. The sky is royal blue, slowly submitting to an invasion of high cirrus clouds.

At the KOA in Winthrop, situated beside a clear, swift-flowing river, we encamp on a soft, dark, finely cut green lawn. This is one of the best campgrounds we have visited, its hosts the most friendly. On the edge of town we dine like royalty in a tastefully appointed restaurant. We both have white wine, stir-fried chicken, vegetables, and rice. The sun is lowering as we leave the air-conditioned restaurant; always a breeze, the 95-degree high is dropping to a more comfortable level. My knee feels normal again. Perhaps I'll try a cautious hike of a mile or two tomorrow in the North Cascades.

DAY NINE
Washington State

Downtown Winthrop is a replica of a typical nineteenth century western town. Tastefully done, its signs and barn wood storefronts are fairly authentic. Attractive restaurants, fancy clothing stores and gift shops line the main street. After our days of traveling in open country, this place is sheer fun. Having had a restful night's sleep, we both awake at 5:50. We find a small 1890s style breakfast spot in town already open, and gobble up a short stack of pancakes with maple syrup, orange juice and coffee. Through a wide storefront window we watch a sudden early morning thundershower flood the street outside.

Winthrop is a good old English name, a good New England name too. When I was a child my parents used to vacation at crowded Winthrop, Massachusetts, where the beach, shielded by a barrier of breakwaters, was rimmed by a seawall and, behind it, a promenade always crowded in the evening with tanned, aged vacationers on a stroll. But a Winthrop in Washington State? How come?

Sure enough, a Massachusetts boy, name of Guy Waring, arrived here back in the 1890s, and named the town after John Winthrop, an early governor of Massachusetts. All of a sudden, I felt mighty kindly about this now memorable place.

During breakfast Danny speaks of his low self-esteem. "I wish I had more confidence," he says. "I wish I could believe in myself more. Why do I feel this way, why? I just can't figure it out."

I have nothing to offer.

Searching himself, he goes on: "Because Ma has

found little satisfaction in her marriage, I think she looked for it in us kids instead, which placed more demands on us than we could meet. I've failed her. And, Dad, you've demanded impossible perfection from us. Nothing we did ever pleased you."

My heart is breaking. He tells me that while he is good at intellectualizing, it gives him no relief. He also feels down, he believes, because he has no woman. Yet a woman would only complicate things. Still, wouldn't she give him the ego reinforcement he needs?

"Take a river for instance," says Danny. "It cuts its own course, goes where it can. It has patience. But dam it up and it'll find a way to defeat the obstacle. A river is real and so is a man."

Route 20, completed as recently as 1972, takes us into North Cascades National Park. From Winthrop the road keeps to a peaceful, pastoral, unspoiled, meandering green valley all the way to the mountains. Narrow, flat, low mountains hem it in on both sides, giving it a cozy charm.

On the mountain road we see deer, some leaping, some standing quietly munching on greens ignoring us, immune to our presence. Again more cyclists appear—in the mountains yet—which continues to astonish me. Yesterday we passed some tandem cyclists. Such courage.

Danny remarks that it is his first time in this part of the country. There's very little of the United States remaining that he hasn't seen.

"Real nice here, real impressive. Have you read Hermann Hesse's *Sidhartha*? No. Well, read it, Dad. You'll enjoy it."

Steep mountains, their sides partially bare, the higher ones snow splotched, are now surrounding us.

"I think I'd like to live in Japan for a year, teach English," Danny says. "They've got their brand of pressures too, different from ours. Their pressure is social—they have to forsake their personal desires and cooperate for the common goal, while we have that drive to succeed as individuals. They have the pressures of an overcrowded community; we have the pressures of lonely independence."

I listened intently and admiringly, for he was speaking from his acute personal observations during a three-month visit to Japan the previous summer.

Unseen by tourists before 1972, the valley narrows under the shadow of jagged, gray rocky spires streaked with snow; gigantic towers—Liberty Bell Mountain, Silver Star Mountain—enclose us more and more tightly as the road twists through hairpin turns. At Washington Pass, 5,500 feet above the sea, it is raining lightly.

After climbing toward the clouds for hours, we pass over the high mountain rim and begin our weaving descent. Below to our right, Ross Lake appears like a dark, deep green amoebae resting between the mountains. It is unexpected, astonishing. Beyond the lake, a cottony white cloud lies abreast two mountain peaks. Surrounded by snowy summits, we cruise in and out of the clouds. The lake below is now pale turquoise and more opaque than the lakes at Glacier, a color no less beautiful.

"These mountains remind me of Japan," Danny says. "I've got to get a picture, especially that color. I've never seen anything like it."

Danny is an expert photographer and does his own developing, including color. His photos of natural scenes, framed and hanging on the walls back home, are poetic; his people pictures are telling character studies. A knowledgeable visitor to our home, expert in judging, has said they are worthy of winning prizes. I am proud of his expertise, humble in the presence of his talent.

The three dams of the Skagit Valley, constructed between 1929 and the early 1960s, are the source of Seattle's electric power. As we progress westward through the steep-sided valley, the rain increases. Small waterfalls plunge from the escarpments beside the road. A sheet-white falls roars through a gorge. Bands of clouds encircle the mountainsides and nestle in the high cirques. The Cascades are wilder, less developed than Glacier, which is often in spots more nearly like a resort.

Emerging from the dense Cascades, the road hugs the tumbling Skagit River. A low fog, formed by warm, moist air lying over the frigid water, hovers above the river which retains the same opaque, pale green color as the lakes in which it is born. Rain is pelting the windshield. An oblivious cyclist passes going uphill. The road enters Marblemont, the first town upon leaving the park, then it passes the Mountain Song restaurant and enters a flat floored valley. Fringing both its sides, what appear to be purple and white wild snapdragons grow in profusion. Road and river head toward the sea for the ncxt sixty miles.

We have breakfast in a town called Concrete, not a replica of the past as was Winthrop, but the real thing, a town that seems hardly changed in a hundred years.

The restaurant, the Village Pantry, is jammed with tables of assorted sizes and shapes. It is crowded with farmers and foresters and layabouts, old and wrinkled, young and smooth, in work clothes and boots. On the walls newspapers blare headlines of old events as if they had just happened: "British Guns Take Huge Jap Toll at Singapore", "Nazi Troops Pass Thru Turk Strait on Way To Syria." Sprinkled among the newspapers are yellowed photos of the town and townspeople from the turn of the century into the 1920s. One shows a tremendous cedar tree dwarfing the men standing beside it.

On a table are stacked a dozen or more photo albums, which I take at random and pore over. There's a picture of the high-school class of '27, another of a man lying stretched across the diameter of a giant cut cedar.

To my question, why the name Concrete, an old farmer joining us at our table says, over a cup of coffee, the town was once the home of the Lone Star Cement Company. Then why not Cement or Lone Star rather than Concrete? Holy cow! Salmon fishing, lumbering, and the manufacture of cedar shingles are the big industries in town now.

"Used to be able to walk across the river on the backs of the salmon," the old farmer says. "Those were great days, great farming. I'm too old for farming now. Oh, they's a few big trees around still. Should be cut else after five hundred, a thousand years they rot and die. But no cutting next to the river ought to be allowed, no sir, that hurts the land."

A sparkling young man parks a bike by the wide restaurant window, enters, and takes the table next to ours. Shyly he answers my questions. A student from Colorado State at Boulder, he has been cycling for three weeks on his eighteen speed. An eighteen speed? Oh, yes, there are twenty-one speed bikes too. He's a loner, does eighty miles a day if the wind and weather are favorable. Heading for Vancouver, then down the coast, he keeps to the mountain passes to avoid the heat, hasn't walked yet, no sir, and doesn't intend to.

"Where you headed?" the forester at the next table asks as Danny and I rise to leave.

"Olympic Peninsula."

"Hey, you'll find enough bullshit there. If there weren't bullshit in the world, it would stop turning," he shouts and everybody laughs and waves goodbye.

We leave town slowly, taking in the old bank and other old buildings, mostly of brick. Not cement?

On our way to the Puget Sound the valley widens, its floor a broad expanse of forest extending left and right to high wooded hills. Some of the hillsides are denuded of their once fine fir trees, a depressing sight. Mom's Place, Home Made Pies, borders the highway.

We are into heavy civilization. In Burlington at Interstate 5 is a sign: "Bachelors have consciences, married men have wives."

Our original plan was to spend a day and an evening with a cousin and his family in Seattle. On phoning to inform them of our impending arrival, a teen-age son answers and says that his parents are on a three week tour of Europe. Danny then proposes that we bypass the crowded metropolitan area and take the ferry across the sound from Whidbey Island to Port Townsend on the Olympic peninsula. Expressing some doubt that we would find space on the ferry, since it is Saturday and the weekenders would be out in force, I go along reluctantly.

Taking Route 20, we drive the twenty miles down Whidbey Island to the ferry only to find my fear confirmed. The jam—hundreds of cars, pickup trucks and RVs—awaiting boarding certainly means that we wouldn't make the ferry then in port, and we couldn't be sure we'd even make the next one four hours later. Abandoning the ferry idea, we decide that taking the interstate through Seattle and rounding the bottom of Puget Sound and up past Bremerton—about 150 miles—would take us no more time than to wait for the next ferry. Back to the mainland we go.

In our haste to make up time, we get lost and find ourselves on a scenic ride along the shore of Puget Sound. How often an unplanned turn onto an unbeaten path proves to be the most rewarding and fun. A lesson in life to be remembered. The countryside is a bucolic, restful scene of rolling, open fields interspersed with small stands of tall fir trees. Marinas filled with pleasure craft are tucked here and there into the shore near small clusters of tastefully designed, gabled, rambling private homes. But these are less common than the boxy, ugly structures that are spread throughout the island.

"Americans lack a real aesthetic sense," I remark. "A well designed new home is a rare thing."

"Yeah," Danny agrees. "We really have lousy taste." Danny's concepts, of course, are influenced by having been part of a crew building well-planned custom homes on Cape Cod.

"When it comes to our entrepreneurial commercial sense, that's where we excel," I add with some regret.

Crossing the graceful bridge spanning the waterway of Deception Pass, which splits the island, we view the open sea down the Juan de Fuca Strait. I had sailed through the strait forty-one years ago aboard the aircraft carrier *Hornet* as a Seabee returning home from the war in the Philippines.

"It was December," I proceed. "After two years in the tropics and still in thin, warm weather clothes, I froze my butt off. First order of business was to get into my warm woolly blues. At my first liberty I high tailed it into downtown Seattle—then much more intimate, more like a small city than it is now—to find a tailor who would clean away the mildew and press the uniform, which was impossibly wrinkled from having been rolled up for so long in my footlocker.

"In that war, returning servicemen were given the royal treatment. While he cleaned and pressed the suit amidst a cloud of steam, I sat shivering in my underwear behind a flimsy curtain. We had a marvelous conversation, which I remember almost word for word: 'Where you from, sailor?' he asked. 'Boston,' I said, even though I was from Worcester (thirty-five miles west of Boston), because in those days no one ever heard of the place despite a population of 200,000. 'Whadya know,' he said. 'Say, you know, we were neighbors before I came out here.' 'No kidding,' I said, thrilled to find someone from around home. 'Whereabouts,' I asked. 'Brooklyn,' he replied, and I couldn't stop laughing. As Einstein says, it's all relative. After asking me what war theater I had served in, since we were once neighbors from the East, he gave me a gift to wear on my blues, the war ribbon that designated service in the Pacific."

We have lunch in a garish Burger King at an unsightly intersection. The Seattle area is frustrating us so far. We are unaccustomed to the heavy traffic. Whidbey Island, simply more of the ugly, commercial mainland for the most part, is a disappointment. Tempted to pass up the Olympic peninsula and "get out of this mess" yet greedy for new natural sights, we hesitate, suspecting that by departing we might miss something worthwhile after all—the northern Pacific beaches, the rain forest.

Still steaming over the time we have lost, I tell Danny that I shouldn't have listened to him, that I should have followed my common sense, which told me the ferry would be a waste of time on a Saturday. I'm kicking myself for not insisting, for not pressing the issue.

"I think we both would have welcomed someone else at the wheel for a change," he replied calmly. "I just never expected any complications—the difference between young optimism and experienced, old skepticism, I guess."

"Well, maybe, but I constantly anticipate the future to avoid inconvenience or disaster," I say annoyed. "That's how I live. That's how I ran my business, else I'd have never succeeded. The ferry situation was exactly as I predicted it would be and we've killed hours of precious time."

As I write my notes on this episode, a voice within persists in asking: But how can I be sure I'm right until I learn by doing? We may have lost precious time but why hurry? Haven't I been hurrying all my life? And now that I'm retired, is it necessary? Was it ever necessary?

"Anyway, what a lousy island," says Danny. "You've got to give it a bad review in your journal."

The sky is overcast and showery; distant mountains are vague in the mist. Driving south on the bustling, wet interstate through metropolitan Seattle, past the skyscrapers and the circular rotating tower, formerly the site of a World's Fair, I reminisce aloud over my last visit to that city with Jane.

She and I, on a leisurely walk around the center of the city, fortuitously entered the huge multistoried atrium of a new office building. At an upper level we sat on a bench gazing down to the main floor on which a boy, perhaps no more than twelve or thirteen, was flawlessly playing the second Rachmaninoff piano concerto on a polished concert grand set on a circular platform in the middle of the floor. Rapt, we listened to the music, which resounded dreamlike throughout the building. We didn't want it to end. When he was done he simply stood and walked away, whereupon a uniformed guard stepped onto the platform and lowered the shiny piano cover over the keys, locked it, and walked away.

We sat lingering for a while in the silent aftermath, still under the spell of the melody. On the way out we met the guard, who explained that the piano was very old and came from a famous, ancient downtown theater that no longer existed. Anyone who was qualified was welcome to come and play. The lad we heard was a frequent visitor and one of the best, a virtuoso. The guard didn't know his name.

When we were in Seattle last, Jane and I were in a happier mode. A hiatus had prevailed in our war of incompatibility. Our hosts, my cousin and his family, showed us the town because, as they said, few relatives visited them stuck up there in the Northwest. We dined at famous fish restaurants and visited exciting art galleries and stores where graceful wood furniture was displayed. We bought a bright woolen Andean area rug for our Cape house.

On a two-day side trip we enjoyed touring Vancouver, staring wide-eyed at the fresh new architecture, ambling through the colorful gardens and the damp redwood forest park, gazing down the bright, wide harbor across to the misty low mountains. From another vantage point in a formal park, we saw the magical skyline of the city. Jane and I agreed that Vancouver is more beautiful than Seattle. "I could live here," I said, a rare admission in view of my dislike of cities.

My cousin's irritable father, my Uncle Harry, in his mid-eighties, just died in a nursing home in Seattle. Uncle Harry is notable and enduring in my memory for a cute story he always told. When he lived in a cottage by a lake in New Hampshire, among a maze of dirt roads, the oil-fired heating boiler failed one December night. Next morning, after showing the repairman the way into the cellar, Uncle Harry stood watching. On sizing up the problem, the repairman reached for a monkey wrench from his kit, and planted a deft blow on a pipe leading to the boiler. Voila, suddenly it worked. Before departing, the repairman left a bill for $97.

Typically, miserable Uncle Harry was indignant. Promptly he mailed the bill back to the repairman with a brief note: "Please itemize."

The bill was returned, itemized as follows:
Travel time to and from place of business,
one hour, $10
Time on customer's premises: 10 minutes, $1.00
Knowing where to strike wrench: $86

We round the southern end of Puget Sound at Tacoma, then travel north through Bremerton, a skeleton steel and asphalt coated shipbuilding city of piers and repair facilities. Quickly after crossing the Hood Canal on a pontoon bridge, we join 101 on the Olympic Peninsula. It is three hours since leaving the ferry terminal on Whidbey Island. The afternoon is dismal. Clouds hide what mountains are visible on the western side of the peninsula.

Reminding us of the Maine coast, the northeast portion of the peninsula has many neglected farms and appears impoverished. Irrigation arrived here at the turn of the century when the land was a desert and cactus bloomed. Only ten to eighteen inches of rain falls here annually, exactly contrary to what we had understood: that the Olympic peninsula is the wettest place on the continent. Of course our information is indeed correct, but it applies to the western side of the peninsula. There, capturing all the rainfall from the moist breezes sweeping in from the Pacific, the Olympic Mountain Range cools off the air on its rise and releases its moisture.

Rather than have to contend with all the wetness by camping out at a KOA, we decide to hole up in a motel in Port Angeles. Driving through the wide streets of this clean, bright, cheery, flag-bedecked town, we check room prices at two AAA-approved motels located on a hilly street overlooking the town and the sea. At $50 to $60, we are outraged. After all, who needs the view? On busy 101 closer to sea level, we find a room for $42 at the Chinook.

On the recommendation of the motel clerk, we dine at a restaurant nearby on the highway, imbibing wine and feasting regally on scrumptious freshly caught halibut. Although the service is rather poor, neither Danny nor I, deep in discussion, mind dallying in the comfortable, pleasant atmosphere. What place could be more congenial? Nevertheless, the waitress, apologizing for the delay, deducts the wine from our bill. We have the certain feeling that everything's going our way.

Our talk centers on the subject of success in terms of values. Earlier Danny had described how the Japanese live in a structured society in which politeness disguises a range of feelings expressed partly through an aggressiveness and drive in group achievement. He has also suggested that a person having low self-esteem thrives in the Japanese social environment because of its custom of politeness toward and respect for each individual, especially strangers and foreigners.

Now in the United States he sees the individual ego as supreme and the pursuit of money, mammon, as the major method and measure of achievement and self-realization.

"Is that what drove you to try to succeed in business to the point that you failed to see that your very survival was at stake?" I ask. Although the tables around us are now buzzing, we easily ignore them.

"Money not worked for, not earned, is worthless so far as I'm concerned," he says. "I must feel good about the money I have. There's no quick way to make money. There's this friend, Benny, who's always looking for a fast buck, a quick deal. He's wrong; it's not the right way, it doesn't satisfy, at least not me.

"You know, when I bought the truck I would have preferred a more low-key color than the red one available. I don't want other people knowing what possessions I have; they would try to take them away from me."

"Because they would envy you? Because you fear their rejection?" I probe. "Or because your sister was born after you and took some of your mother's love away from you?"

Staring into my eyes he shrugs and I sip more wine.

"Let me tell you about success," I go on. I tell of our friends the Binders—Biff and Betty and their six children.

"Fresh from high school Biff started out with a small snack restaurant on wheels, which he stationed at strategic places around the city during different times of the day. After a couple of years, he bought another mobile snack bar, and six months later a third. Eventually he secured concessions in public parks and on college campuses and owned a small fleet of mobile bars.

"The money flooded in, all cash, which, since there was no record of sales transactions, enabled Biff to evade taxes. Over the years he and Betty bought their dream house, drove big Lincoln Continentals, hired gardeners, cleaning help, and a nanny. They could have lived still higher, except that Biff preferred to hide his wealth to avoid arousing the suspicions of the IRS. Instead they spent their money on non-material things, such as weekends in Bermuda, the entire family, all eight of them. They went on clothes-buying trips to Hong Kong and nightclub jaunts to Paris. Afraid to stash his money away in banks or even safe deposit boxes for fear of discovery, he felt compelled to spend it. Maybe he put some in Swiss banks, but he never said so. Freely confiding in me, he seemed under compulsion to tell somebody of his success, to show off somehow, this man with only a high-school education.

"When he was in his early forties, at a time of life when most men make a change, have one last reach for the stars, either then or never, he sold his profitable fleet of snack bars and invested the entire proceeds in a posh downtown restaurant. It was a glamorous place with a pianist, and a sexy coat girl, and a hostess with an English accent.

"But downtown was dying. After 5 o'clock when the office workers and their bosses left for home, they had no desire to return before the next morning. If they went shopping after dinner, or had dinner out, they went to the suburban all-weather indoor malls.

"Biff refused to see that his restaurant had actually

croaked at the starting gate, and he wouldn't give up. After exhausting his own cash, he borrowed from banks, poured more money into the restaurant, and built a fancier bar; he hired more exciting entertainment—expensive trios and singers for instance—and a famous cook from Paris. Then the banks said "enough," so he put the touch on his friends, myself included. Contributing a part of our then small savings, I never really expected to get it back. He was blind to the truth of his dilemma. Hadn't he always succeeded? Hadn't his life been on an upward curve ever since he was eighteen? Consistent success breeds its own arrogance. He gambled all on one horse, didn't hedge, because, never having been humbled by life, he believed he was favored by fate, infallible.

"When tragedy struck, it was total. Betty, suddenly afflicted with breast cancer, was operated on. Six months later Biff's lung had to be removed. The restaurant went belly-up. They were evicted from their dream home; all their furniture and belongings were moved from the house to the lawn and auctioned off from under them. Their humiliation was total, almost unendurable."

"That's terrible! What did they do then?" Danny's jaw was agape.

"For a while they lived with friends. Most of their relatives washed their hands of them. After all, their monetary contributions went down the drain too. Some of their friends behaved as if they were ashamed of them. So they left the state, their past, and their friends, and slowly Biff started again in a small way while Betty went to work waitressing. Now, a few years later, they are recovering nicely; they have since repaid my loan to them. They are wiser human beings than before, and I believe richer for being poorer."

Danny becomes thoughtful. Compared with Biff's failure, his own recent one was small. But does he see that it contained the same ingredients, the same blind belief in success, the same refusal to cut bait and save the rest of the line?

"Life is like riding a wave," I say. "Sometimes the period is long, but sooner or later what's up comes down and vice versa. You are right in wanting to earn success. However, to preserve it, anticipate failure. In that respect I have always been humble: Never expecting success, I can't believe I've arrived. Your mother feels the same way. She's very conservative."

"Maybe that's where I get it from," Danny says.

"Maybe. She likes frugality and dislikes display. Her ways are judicious. With her I'm comfortable."

Not so, I think, the woman who was my mistress. She loved dressing to the nines, showing off, spending money as if there were no tomorrow. She used to call me cheap because I spent cautiously. Her ways frightened me.

"Your mother and I have reached the stage where we want to simplify our lives. Possessions have come to mean less and less. What counts now are relationships."

After the check arrives (with the wine charge crossed off) we leave the restaurant to wash our clothes in the laundry at the motel. A motel laundry is a prime place for meeting people and talking, almost as good as a bar. A young South Dakota couple just returned from the Vancouver Expo tell of being discouraged by the long lines; between 10 a.m. to 10 p.m. each day they had visited only two or three exhibits. The man inquires about what to see in Seattle; Danny recommends the lively restored waterfront, which he knew from a previous visit, and gives directions on getting there. Weary, Danny retires to our room while I wait for the dryer to finish its cycle.

After the young couple leaves, I become bored and go to our room to find out how Danny is doing. I find him sleeping soundly on the bed cover with his clothes on. Returning to the laundry, I encounter an old couple, a rotund, wheezing old man seated in a sagging aluminum lawn chair and his cold looking, gray haired wife bending over the top loading washing machine.

"You been to the Expo?" the old man demanded.

"No sir."

"Big rip-off. Lines hours long. Never been to a World's Fair before, sorry I went to this one, and never will go to one again. But that's what my son wanted, so I went along. He's twenty-eight and still not married. You married?"

"Yes sir, I'm here with my son, too."

I'm apprehensive that the chair will collapse as it creaks ominously when the old man shifts. His wife stands by the washer listening, approvingly.

"From Nebraska, we are. Have a 160 acre farm, which I rent out. Too old to do it myself now. Used to work in the oil fields when I was young. Used to be county commissioner. Not bad, I'd say, right Ma? Your son married?"

His gray haired, quiet wife suddenly leaves the tiny laundry room.

"No sir."

"Well, neither is mine. A good boy, though, the very best. Guess he's just plain not ready."

His wife returns and stands before him embarrassed

and befuddled. "Seems I don't remember which room we're in," she says.

The old man smiles, gently reminding her, "Third one on the right sweet. OK?" She nods and after she leaves, he says sadly, "She's very forgetful these days, worse than her old man."

Is she a victim of Alzheimer's? I wonder. I suspect the old man is worried. For sure, he's a self-centered old man. Then why do I find myself so sympathetic?

"Where you from?" he demands again.

"Massachusetts."

"Hell, I know Massa—whateveryoucallit—like the back of my hand. Stationed at Miles Standish Army Base near . . . what's that town?"

"Taunton. The base is an industrial park now."

"Yup, spent a week there before debarking for Europe. Traveled all over Europe, fought in France after D Day. That was a war to be proud of. Where you going from here?"

"The rest of the peninsula, Hoh rain forest."

"I'm letting my son plan the trip. He wants to see the redwoods down near San Francisco, so that's where we're going."

His wife returns again just as I am folding our clothes from the dryer. With his heaviness the old man has difficulty rising from the rickety chair. We shake hands and say good-bye.

Turning on the TV in our room, I get a news program without commercials on a Vancouver station, less sensational and seemingly more objective than our news broadcasts. Danny awakens, annoyed with the sound of the TV, and orders me to shut it off.

I sleep until 4:30, roused by a dream about Jane, myself, and friends, another married couple. They are, in real life, friends who were divorced from previous spouses and introduced to each other by my wife. We four, seated together in a movie theater, cannot see the screen from our location. As a consequence they are not interested in the movie, but I am and move to another seat to watch alone. Troubled by the dream, I speculate that it depicts my alienation from Jane, and my desire to leave her.

DAY TEN
Olympic Peninsula, Washington

Awaking to low clouds, we take off skeptically for the visitors' center at Hurricane Ridge, the favored spot from which to view the mountains. As expected, the clouds obscure the view so we head west on 101. The road circles long, narrow, turquoise, alpine Lake Crescent, flanked by two-to-three thousand foot high forested hills. As the road leaves the park, a land denuded of its once enormous cedars and hemlocks extends for miles—a wasteland of stumps and underbrush. We are saddened by the desecration.

"Why is this allowed? How can we be so stupid as not to require replanting?" I mutter.

Missing a turn, Danny gets us lost again. I insist on backtracking the few miles we have gone and not make the same mistake we made yesterday. When he becomes instantly defensive, I decide not to press the issue. He almost goes through a red light, the second time in two days, but I hold my tongue. Sensing that a small strain has developed between us, I do my damnedest to contain it.

The road to La Push leads through more stripped, un-replanted land. Beer bottles and beer cases lie strewn along the road shoulders for most of its eight-mile length to the sea.

"It seems humanity has uglified a large part of this otherwise naturally beautiful peninsula," I say dismayed.

But the hard, wide, gray-brown sandy beach at LaPush is gloriously unspoiled. The cool sea-scented air is like a caress. A gentle surf curls between rough vertical rock islands, natural castles floating on the sea. Some of the islands are forested, others barren. Some are lone, thin fingers, others broad and hulky.

With childlike pleasure, I watch the sea surge between a narrow opening beneath a natural rock bridge. It makes a thick, sucking sound. Danny calls to me to see a brilliant orange and dark purple starfish clinging to a barnacle-laden rock. Gently poking a stick into the core of the light green anemones, we are intrigued as they enclose the shaft with their short tentacles. Carrying our shoes, we walk along the edge of a deep, crystalline, green tidal pool.

Behind us, a wide ribbon of ancient stumps and naturally felled trees, bleached silver, separates the thick tree line from the beach. Strewn haphazardly, as if by a Jack in the Beanstalk giant that had played pick-up-sticks, some of the downed trees are well over a hundred feet long, four to six feet in diameter. The cloudy sky, except for scattered streaks of white, is pewter, like the sandy beach. Wanting to touch the Pacific, I choose a spot behind a castle island where the surf is restrained; I lay my hand flat against the transparent water. It is not as cold as I expect, not as frigid as the Atlantic at Nauset on Cape Cod.

Returning by way of the path that brought us there, we take a stairway that zigzags for several hundred feet up the steep verdant forested incline rising from the beach. The path runs for three-quarters of a mile through a dense rain forest of hemlock. Underfoot the path is spongy. The dank earth is abundant with graceful ferns, old rotting stumps, and fallen tree trunks from which new trees, tall and twisting, are reaching for light. From the stuff of the old and weak grow the new and strong.

Ahead Danny stops to light up. I see he is smoking more and more as our journey progresses. He has tried to quit often, he says again. As I suspected at the beginning of our trip, I feel sure now he has a self-destructive impulse. If he'd like to have psychotherapy, I repeat my willingness to pay for it. Yes, he reassures me, he is eager to take "the road less traveled," referring to Scott Peck's book of that name. I had read it the previous winter at his suggestion. Through therapy he'll find the way to love himself, I say, and establish a sense of self-worth.

At Forks a banner across the highway reads: "Ya'll Come Back Now."

"I will, I will," Danny shouts, proclaiming his desire to revisit the Olympic Peninsula someday.

The long road to the Hoh rain forest passes through more scenes of forest destruction. The Hoh itself is a marvel of 250 foot spruces. Hemlocks, Douglas fir, cedar, and maples (in sunny places) acquire a magnitude attained no where else. Under the dense canopy the forest light is suffused, the air naturally cooled (nature's air-conditioning) and sweetly pine scented. A mass of ferns blankets the forest floor. The extended limbs of maples, stretching like gnarled beggars' arms, are shrouded in green moss. In the Hoh it rains 140 inches a year, creating an unimaginable place.

While taking the half-hour hike (longer ones are possible) through the primeval reservation, I tell Danny of my long persistent wish to visit this peninsula. On this path I have found what I came for. Feeling lightheaded and without substance as within a dream, I am bowled over by the fantasy forest.

"So what do you think of the place, now that you're here," Danny asks on the way out.

"It all depends. Wherever man is, I see devastation. But where he isn't, where he's kept away, it's as impressive and beautiful as I expected. The clear-cutting saddens me."

"Still we need the resources," Danny argues. "Where

else can we find this kind of lumber, especially for making shingles?"

"Don't get me wrong. I agree that people are important and we must use what the land provides in order to survive, but only temporarily. Future generations will also need the earth's yield, so let's replant and restore, yes, even improve. And let each generation during its tenure bear the cost of restoration by including it in the price of things."

Danny listens and nods.

South of the Hoh on 101 along the western side of the peninsula, the road tunnels through a towering corridor of thick hemlocks. It's a road through an eternal ancient forest, a road through forever. We stop for lunch at a highway restaurant that overlooks the Pacific, and eat fried oysters, tender and fresh. Unhappily forsaking the bewitching peninsula, we move on, and soon enter a flat, dull countryside that evolves into the blighted outlying streets of a commercial, industrial metropolitan area.

Heavy traffic crams I-5 to Olympia, capital of the state. After registering at a KOA near Olympia, we have a yen for Italian food and head back to town. Searching up and down the clean, wide, downtown streets, currently abandoned for the evening, we choose an old gas station that has been cleverly renovated to serve as a restaurant, the Casa Mia, cheerful in buff and orange and white. The overhead doors to what were formerly greasing bays have been retained and still work. The dinner was first-rate Italian; we congratulate ourselves on so lucky a choice.

Over dinner we discuss Danny's concerns about his future. He had slept restlessly last night in the motel at Port Angeles and had ground his teeth. When I had awakened from my dream at 4:30 a.m. he too was awake.

"I guess I'm afraid," Danny had said, lying on the next bed in the pitch dark. "I'm afraid of the near future, of therapy, of finding a new place to live, of a new job. I'm just afraid."

Getting down to specifics at dinner, I tell Danny that a commission sales job, which he was considering, would be folly because of its uncertain income.

No argument, he says, and brings the subject back to how he feels. "You know what causes me to feel worthless? When I see a young couple. Not having a girl gets me down."

"But having a girl only compounds the problem, Danny. You must work on what's bothering you first before taking on the responsibility of a relationship."

"I know you're right, that having a girl is a kind of false cure, still, I also know she would reinforce my sense of self-worth."

Since neither his point nor mine sticks, I make a practical suggestion. "Say, don't you think it's time we saw a movie?" He brightens. "How about *Back to School* with Rodney Dangerfield? It's showing at a shopping center in Lacey."

Coincidentally the movie is set in Madison, Wisconsin, at the university we visited a week earlier. We are excited at recognizing scenes of the campus and the lake. A spoof of college life concerning the relationship between a father and son, it makes us laugh throughout. Audaciously indulging in fakery, exaggerating the triumph of appearance over substance, it delivers a message ironically apropos to many of our talks. Having fun and laughing together seem to cleanse us of our differences. We are soaring as we leave the theater.

"It's good to break the routine once in a while, right Danny?"

"We break it so much these days, breaking it has become routine."

We laugh some more.

"Last night, halibut at a fancy place; tonight spaghetti in a gas station; tomorrow the world. This is living, Danny."

As we pull into the KOA to finally sleep for the night, Danny shouts, "Look, Dad, over there."

Following his gaze I see snowcapped Mount Rainier hovering in the flat, clear distance two hours away.

"Rainier's 14,000 feet; Fuji's only 12,000," my world-traveling son exclaims.

DAY ELEVEN
Washington & Oregon

At the large truck-stop restaurant near the interchange on I-5 we devour a Paul Bunyan breakfast. Our conversation borders on the erudite. We discuss the danger of overpopulating the world, the folly of not limiting our numbers, and the decline of quality of life by not doing so. We discuss the good and bad effects of technology, on the one hand improving our lot and on the other harming us when it becomes an end in itself.

Visiting the men's room before leaving, I read among the wall graffiti, "Fuck off. Die all you faggots. I'll stay with pink pussy." Below a reply: "Amen." And below that, "Must have been a nigger wrote this." The walls speak, representing the moral level of the men who pass by here. Reading the walls I lose hope, at least for now.

After breakfast Danny asks me to take the wheel on the road to Rainier. The mountain, standing silent, snow laden above all else, performing its own solitary show, is a hypnotic beacon.

"It's more dramatic than the other great mountains I've seen," Danny says. "Even Whitney."

Stopping at a viewing point off the highway, we stare at the blown away north-face of Mount St. Helens, thirty or forty miles off to the south. A swaying quilt of tall purple and white bell-shaped flowers covers the field below us. The sky is bright, the air sweet and bracing, the world a joy.

When Rainier is nearer and larger, we pull off the road to absorb its grandeur and to photograph each other with the mountain as a backdrop. Soon the road slices through a shadowy forest of giant fir trees whose girth and height are comparable to those in Hoh. Remnants of snow survive in the shady spots. Zigzagging, the thin road climbs along ledges chiseled from the sheer mountain walls, occasionally widening just enough to allow parking for a view.

We meet a couple from Paris traveling with their young children. He is tall, trim, smartly handsome; she is shining and freshly beautiful. We talk of the recent U.S. bombing of Libya, of which he heartily approved.

"But your government objected to what we did," I say.

"Officially, yes," he says in accented, precise English, "but it is not advertised that France really allowed the U.S. fighters to fly across the French Pyrenees on the way to Libya."

Although skeptical of his claim, I remember when I was in Paris in May, a waiter commented that the French people admired Reagan's no-nonsense aggressiveness. And isn't that a reason why a majority of the American people voted for him too?

Continuing the twisting climb, we are surrounded by a vast rim of snowy peaks, of which Ranier is the highest. We are traversing the nucleus of a great caldera.

To think that Rainier is an afterthought, not in our original itinerary. And I conveniently forget my insistence that we plan every move in advance.

"Rainier is a stupendous bonus, Danny," I say.

"The unexpected isn't such a bad thing after all," he says, grinning.

Touché, I think.

"Agreed. Actually the unexpected is what makes life so interesting. Without it, life would be a bore."

And the unexpected erupts everywhere. The scenery is outrageously mad; Rainier's rich green flanks rocket into a blue sulphate sky; jagged columns of rock claw the air with their snow mantled tips; Mount Adams's perfect cone pokes up in a surprise showing from behind lower heights; in deep, dusky verdant canyons, thin rivers of tinsel flash in the sun. All is beyond expectation, un-exceeded in spectacle by any scenery we have witnessed so far.

At the un-crowded circular visitor center we stare through plate glass at Rainier's many glaciers, at its mysterious, treacherously silent white summit. The literature says 2,500 people a year climb Rainier.

"And why?" I ask.

"Because it's there," we shout together.

"Time to go, Dad. There's a lot more to see."

This is the largest vertical mass I have set eyes upon. Spellbound, I must rip myself away.

On the way down, drawn to look back, I watch Rainier's white-spattered east face bursting into the cobalt sky behind us. Rainier's scale—its sister mountains, the valleys, the vast walls of green—is greater than Glacier's or North Cascade's.

The further we descend, the fatter and taller the trees become, the damper the air. Not to forget, to enjoy again, like a camera, my eyes take snapshots of a splash of tall, slender flowers, a dappled forest of gigantic fir trees, a carpet of chartreuse moss. A deer with two fawns bound across the road. We are happy with this world.

We pass Rim Rock Lake, formed by a dam, a large, long expanse of calm green water imprisoned between high wooded hills. We are headed for Yakima, Washington.

"Are there yaks in Yakima?" Danny wonders.

"Oh, no," I reply, "but there are kimas there. Say, are we or aren't we still going downhill?"

"Gosh, Dad, can't you see we're level, staying with the lake."

"That proves nothing. Hell, the lake could be going downhill."

Oh, yes, we are. We are most pleased with this world.

I am pleased with my son, with his company, with my love for him.

"This is a true transcontinental pickup truck," Danny says fondly. "She's crossed the country back and forth."

"Yup. You're amazing. At your tender age, you've traveled the face of the earth. What remains now is to travel within yourself."

"I think we had a fascinating breakfast conversation this morning," says Danny.

"Well, I do too."

"In your journal are you going to reveal that I'm all fucked up?" he asks.

"No one will know. I'll use a fake name, a nom de plume. Hey, why don't I call myself Norman Daplume?"

We are free spirits gliding down Route 12 beside a white-water river laughing together. Our mood is outrageously silly.

"We've lisped in Twisp, and pissed in Pyscht. As with a Toyota, could we ask for anything more?"

Life this very moment is full as we enter a fresh new world. It is a high desert of barren hillsides and columns of basalt carved from an ancient lava bed—the result of a great explosion eons ago when a cone that existed blew apart and became the caldera of which Rainier is a part. Layers of congealed lava tower a thousand feet above us. Groves of deciduous trees pack the valley between barren brown and light orange basalt hillsides. Cylinders of basalt are definable in the high cliff walls. The earthscape bares its soul; the violence of its history is like a frozen shout.

Finding my hat soaking wet in the rubble behind the seat, I think, God, what a slob Danny is. The stashing area behind our seats is a mess. The sleeping section is a mess. When seeking something, he throws things about, increasing the disorder and making me uncomfortable. But again, knowing how fragile his self-esteem is, I hold back, say nothing.

To keep track of my possessions I conduct periodic searches, for nothing remains where I last deposited it. My hat got soaked when he tossed his leaking water bottle into the stashing area. Diplomatically I tell him how important order is, especially in business. He claims to know where everything is, that what is disorder to me is not so to him, that it's all a point of view. It's an argument I know I won't win.

"What do you know? Apple orchards in the high desert." And on a bountiful flat green strip along the Yakima River grape vineyards thrive.

Intriguing are the colorful names of western towns and counties: Gleed, Selah, Klickitat County, Walla Walla, and, earlier on the way to Rainier, Mossy Rocky. Here's Horse Heaven Hills.

"Where all dead horses go," I say, feebly attempting to be funny.

Around us the low hills are brown, yellow, and dry. From U.S. 97, white-splotched Rainier sixty to seventy miles away ascends into the clear horizon. We see the whole mountain and make out the tree line. Whereas the sky was unsullied blue when we were there, now in the late morning, clouds hover over the broad peak. Truly, Rainier makes its own weather.

We arrive in Toppenish. Seeing that our gas gauge reads two-thirds empty, I suggest we stop for gas.

"We won't encounter any large towns for about two hundred miles and small towns usually charge more. Here the price is right: ninety-five cents a gallon."

"I think we stop too often," says Danny in annoyance. "You want to stop even when we're half full."

"Hell, you're the one who suggests most of the stops—for viewing, and at fruit stands," I counter. "You make these stops to smoke because you know I won't allow it in the cab."

A silence falls between us, the false calm of a storm brewing.

At 1:30 in the afternoon, tooling along US 97 through Satus Pass, a wooded height in the desert, Danny suggests we take any random road off the highway in search of a place to picnic.

"No," I say. "Better a roadside rest or a public picnic area."

"Why not?" he fumes. "It's more fun to get off the beaten path."

"A road off the highway would probably be private out here. I don't like invading private property."

"I do it often. I don't bother anybody and no one bothers me."

The atmosphere in the truck cab is thick with tension. After driving in angry silence for a short while, Danny pulls into a state camping area, an oasis. Will it be an oasis for our emotions too? Danny sets up his small gas camping stove on the tailgate, but he can't find his lighter in the chaos behind the truck seat. Although tempted to rub it in, I withhold commenting. Yes, I admit he's not totally disorganized. And maybe he'll improve by the time he's back in his own business, else he'll pay dearly. Maybe he'll eventually see the advantage of keeping things orderly. Finally, finding a book of matches elsewhere he lights the stove and boils water for soup.

During lunch we have it out again. Danny won't drop it.

"You have a closed mind, Dad."

"I repeat, I don't like going down strange roads or trespassing on private property. Furthermore we can't afford detours because I thought we agreed that we'd try to cover as much ground as possible today. Tomorrow should be more leisurely. Didn't we plan it that way because we expect to be up late tomorrow night with our friends in Davis? Anyway, I figured a campground or rest area would show up."

"Which proves you aren't adventuresome," he says arrogantly. "I gave in to you since I knew a state park was coming up from looking at the map."

"Well, I missed it on the map. But don't you think this is a pleasant place, better than some chance spot where we might be intruding?"

"We wouldn't be intruding. It's a big, empty land."

Seeing we are at a stalemate, my anger mounts, especially at his persistence. In a long shouting harangue, I voice my disgust with his general disorder.

"In our small quarters what you call disorder is unavoidable," he answers coldly. "And I've told you I know where everything is."

"Like a squirrel looking for last season's nuts after an

earthquake," I say.

"What's the harm in it? Why does it get to you so?"

"For one thing, didn't my hat get soaked?"

"Are you blaming me for that? How can you prove I'm responsible?" His voice has a controlled cold edge to it, his outward appearance is contained. That's his way with anger. In contrast I become excited and loud.

"Not specifically, except I know it's a result of your disdain for neatness. Look, I suggest we end this. It's getting us no place. We're at an impasse. We'll never see eye to eye. Let's drop it once and for all."

I walk away; the rift becomes physical. Yards apart, each of us eats painfully by himself.

We end lunch with fresh cherries, pears, and nuts. On returning to the cab, he searches again for his lost lighter and admits sheepishly that the place behind the seats is a mess. His manner is conciliatory.

Leaving the park, we suddenly see cone-shaped, snow-covered Mount Hood looming straight ahead through the trees about sixty miles distant.

"Mount Hood looks more like Fuji," he says.

For the first time we see the beginning of the mountain string. Framing the horizon north and south in a single view, we see flat-topped Mount Adams (12,700 feet) and pyramid-shaped Mount Hood (11,200 feet).

In response to Danny's revised attitude, I decide to thrash out the gas-buying episode.

"I want to apologize for Toppenish. I should have spoken less sharply. I got mad when you ignored my suggestion to stop and just kept driving on. As I said, I knew we'd have to pay more for gas in the smaller towns down the line. It's the same old planning-ahead syndrome rearing it's ugly head again. Danny, I had sensible reasons for opposing you. But I want your friendship and love."

Figuratively we kissed and made up and felt good again.

A considerable distance downstream from our last transit, we cross the Columbia River for the third and last time. From our barren hilly height, a smooth new road winds to a high, graceful white concrete bridge. Looking down river from the bridge, we are stunned by the sight of snowy Mount Hood rising above a golden hill. A long line of semi-trailer trucks crawling the up-grade into the smooth hills on the south side of the river slows our entrance into Oregon. Fields of brilliant golden wheat, silhouetted against a deep blue heaven, greet us as we climb. The rolling hills embracing the highway are a patchwork of russet, dark green, pale green, and yellow. Portions of the enormous rich brown earth are freshly planted.

Near Grass Valley the mountains line up again: in one vista from south to north, the magnificent white hulks of Jefferson, Hood, Adams, and Rainier, pierce the horizon. A film of high, thin clouds coats the light blue sky.

The names of Oregon's towns are also picturesque: Biggs, Wasco, Grass Valley, Shaniko (population 40), Terrebonne, Bend.

The cultivated land gives way to desert. Adding to the lineup, North Sister shows on the horizon poking above the chaparral. We cross the 45th parallel, the halfway point between the equator and the North Pole.

"It feel's different already," I joke. The strain has disappeared; humor is back and welcome. Pausing at a "snow-cap identifier stop," a brass marker in concrete, in the desert just below the 45th, we join some tourists to view the entire lineup: Rainier, Adams, Mount St. Helens, Hood, Jefferson, Three Finger Jack, Washington, Three Sisters, Broken Top.

We congratulate ourselves on taking Route 97, another uncommonly fortuitous choice (Route 2 in North Dakota was the other), for we had no idea it would be so breathtaking, so rich in color, topography, fragrance, drama.

Farther south, approaching Madras, the land is a patchwork crop of green against the immense backdrop of Mount Jefferson and the Three Sisters. Everywhere irrigation geysers swirl their watery nebulae across the hot fields. The clouds are thickening; the air is fiery and dry.

In recent days we have played the radio and tapes less often. Perhaps it's a distraction and we'd rather absorb the changing scenery unadulterated by other sensations. Despite our differences, our petty crises, I feel, in sharing our experience, Danny and I are also developing an intense new closeness.

Below Madras a pungent odor wafts from the dark green fields into our scorching, breeze-filled cab.

"It smells like tomatoes," I yell above the wind beating in our ears. "Look, tomato plants growing."

Beyond the flat cultivated fields to our left are the arid desert slopes of low hills; to our right in the faraway distance is a hazy blue mountain range, broken by Jefferson's white peak and the Three Sisters. Near Redmond, a high bridge crosses a deep, narrow canyon; a blue streak of water courses through its bed.

"I don't see this on the map," I complain.

"Let's write Rand McNally, inform them it's here," Danny suggests.

This evening a KOA (in Bend, Oregon) has never

been more welcome. We are exhausted from an overfull day. The campground, located right off the highway on a grassy flat, has a grocery store, gas station, extensive shower facility, and phones. By 7:00 p.m. the hot breeze becomes tolerable. On an air-conditioned verandah at a nearby Steak & Brew, we have a dinner of top sirloin steak for $7.95—my first beef in a year of almost vegetarianism—and all the beer we can drink. Relaxed, loosened by the beer, Danny and I talk freely.

"I think I know why my self-esteem is so low," he confesses. "I think it's because I'm two people with two conflicting forces within myself. My inner being has assumed a kind of dichotomy. And I'm this way because my parents are in conflict and represent two ways of behaving. You're aggressive and Ma's submissive."

"Do you really think your mother is so passive?"

"Well, sometimes she is and sometimes she isn't. When it comes down to it, she's a pretty resolute woman."

The subject is engrossing, our talk zealous.

"Am I really that aggressive?"

"Sometimes yes, sometimes, no."

"Under my bluster, you would probably find a secretly passive man."

"Possibly, possibly."

"I think in therapy you'll find out whether you're right or not," I say encouragingly. "I'm sure you'll find some surprises on the road to self-discovery."

Convinced that he doesn't know what he thinks, I hold back saying that I think all his talk is intellectualizing, that he's seeking superficial answers as a substitute for the deeper truth.

During my turn in the shower room (while Danny guards our gear), I overhear two men in conversation.

"I'm from North Carolina, Raleigh. Where you from?" The voice is young.

"Around here."

"We've been traveling across the country for more than a month."

"Yeah? I'm not traveling far. How long you staying?"

"Couple days. Looking to put down roots out here. Heard there's enormous opportunity."

"Yeah, what do you do?"

"Electronics technician. Raleigh's getting crowded. Too much traffic, too much development. There are more Ph.D.s in Raleigh than anywhere else in the world. If you don't have a Ph.D. forget it."

"Whatcha gonna do here?"

"Get out of analogue and into digital. Computers, you know."

"Yeah, that's the coming thing."

I chuckle to myself: Hasn't the computer industry long since reached maturity?

"Well, you know analogue. FM. It's over. Know what FM means? Fuckin' magic."

"Ha, ha. Good luck."

"Sure thing. You too."

I feel sad yet hopeful for the young voice. Another young man having it rough. Since both men leave before I open the door to my stall, I never see them. But the voices are enough.

While Danny showers and I'm alone at our grassy campsite guarding the gear, I sit at a nearby picnic table writing in the journal. I observe a young woman at the site next door labor at setting up a pyramidal pup tent. Soon her husband, returning from his ablutions, struggles to finish the job. Her face turns blue as she attempts and fails to blow up an air mattress. Her husband tries, has no better luck, and gives up.

Meanwhile a middle-aged couple with a garish motorbike dragging a small trailer make camp across the way. They install a fancy tent over the trailer and establish a small kitchen of elegant chrome cooking devices on the lawn. Offering beers to the inept couple next door, they say they are Canadians, old hands at traveling, having recently covered more than five thousand miles since leaving Halifax, Nova Scotia, where they were caught in rain for five days. The couple next door confess that this is their first camping trip. No kidding, say the Canadians. No kidding, think I.

I must sort out my thoughts about Danny. I realize he has hurt me by stubbornly attacking what I am. "I am closed minded. I am not adventuresome." He fights nasty. Still, no doubt he is right, no doubt I miss many opportunities. I'm not against reforming myself: Indeed my own road less traveled has led me to consider new ways of behavior.

Haven't I, in arguing with Danny, defended my decisions and desires strictly on a rational basis? Wouldn't his disorderly ways have more serious negative consequences someday? Under no circumstances have I criticized what he is, only what he does that interferes with my comfort and well being. Yet he may have taken my obstinacy as a personal attack. I find this very sad. He is often too insecure for me to deal with.

I had dreaded the trip from the very beginning. The sights I have seen have surpassed my imagination, but what I see in Danny I'd rather not have seen at all.

DAY TWELVE
Oregon & California

Last night before retiring I called my friend Carl in Davis to advise him of our expected arrival time tonight. With a big convention in town and unexpected guests taking up Carl's and Irene's only spare bedroom, Carl suggests we book a spot right away at the KOA outside Sacramento. They'll expect us for a barbecue at their house by 7:00 p.m. or earlier.

Next I called Fred and his wife, cousins who live in San Rafael outside San Francisco. We planned to visit them tomorrow and had so informed them in a card I had sent from Indiana. Although Danny has visited more recently, I haven't seen them for several years.

"I don't get home from work until 7:30, and Janice has a class until 8:00," Fred warned. "We can get together after that."

"Seeing you so late, we wouldn't have much time to spend together, Fred. We shut eyes by ten to get an early morning start. And frankly we'd have to hang around the whole day waiting because we'll only be coming from Davis. I think we'd better pass it up."

"Hell, even a couple of hours, Harry, is something."

"I know, I know. But there'll be other times."

"We'd really like to see you."

"Yeah and we feel the same way. It just won't work. I'm sorry. Next time, Fred, next time."

Apparently miffed, he hung up. On weeknights it's difficult to see working people. (Fred is an attorney and works late.) Am I taking my retirement freedom for granted? Yes, I'll write Fred and Janice, tell them that since Jane and

I plan to winter for a while next year on the West Coast, we'll make arrangements to spend a weekend with them then. I'm uneasy about the episode, miffed too that Fred wasn't more accommodating to our schedule.

At last in familiar country, having prepared a "great" tour of eastern California for me, Danny becomes enthusiastic. Last night we resolved to get away at least by 6:30 a.m. in order to absorb the countryside more leisurely and perhaps arrive at Carl's early to relax. Instead, Danny sleeps until 6:30. Knowing his weariness, I choose not to wake him.

He's much more laid back than I. Truth is I could never take it easy. Don't I always have to have a pot boiling? So I wait for Danny with forced patience as I have waited for years for his slow paced mother.

Danny has awakened in an irritable, depressed mood. Indeed at times I don't enjoy his company. Given the choice at this moment, I would have the journey over, finis. I would rather be in my study relearning what I have forgotten these past two weeks about how to use my brand-new word processor. I'm anxious to get on with writing and feeling productive. Haven't I already seen enough to last a few years, a lifetime?

At the outset, hadn't I feared the trip might be too long? But Danny insisted we would need all the time he allotted and then some. Nor did we follow his preferences: side trips along strange, uncharted roads, or stopping in any clearing by a stream and swimming in the nude, or the type of spontaneous events that had occurred on his trip east with Pam. As a consequence we have made better time than expected.

Certainly my ways have inhibited him. Because of

me, he can't abandon himself to the moment; he can't express his natural youthful zest. We are a contrast of styles, of generations, of chronological ages. I need the security of anticipating the future; he needs the stimulation of not knowing the future. I am staid, he is daring. He loves life. Am I possibly afraid of it? Something is deeply wrong between us, something concerning our different views of the world. Blind to his needs, I stubbornly reject another way, his way. A wall stands between us and it's mine.

The Oregon road from Bend to Crater Lake streaks monotonously flat and straight through a dead and dying pine forest. Is this forest a victim of the same insect that has devastated vast stands of pines in Washington State, where notices are posted informing of the blight? Ahead to our right, snow-capped Diamond Peak and Mount Thielsen rise from amid the pale blue Cascade Range.

We turn right onto Route 138, deserted, smoothly paved, the entrance to the piney Crater Lake area. Then we drive about twenty-five miles, turn left, and start our rise to the lake itself. The day is clear as glass. Snowdrifts still survive on the more sheltered southern apron of the curving, ascending road. I'm driving, tempted to stop and have fun in a snowball fight with Danny, but I resist the impulse.

Crater Lake, a five-mile wide pit filled with water, is what remains of a former volcano that blew its top. Clinging to the rim of the lake at several spots, the road provides unobstructed views of the enormous scene, which extends for miles to distant mountains. Because of its depth and consequent coldness, the lake assumes a unique navy blue hue, enhanced by a surrounding backdrop of glistening, snow splotched peaks.

From our height at the rim, the view of the expanse is panoramic. We are deceived into underestimating the lake's enormous magnitude until a tour boat, holding a hundred people and appearing like a child's toy, moves in slow motion. It leaves behind a wake of miniature ripples in the shape of a half-closed fan. In the west a cloud bank hovers above the lower mountain ranges and close to the sea; according to the radio it's raining on the coast. To the north are white-cloaked Mount Thielsen and Mount McLoughlin; to the south another sheeted pyramid. The breeze is cool, steady, and pristine, the air diamond clear, the heaven more darkly blue than the lake, the silence vast. We are in touch with eternity. The day is perfect for being here, for being alive, for being together.

At one viewing point a couple from San Antonio raves over the scene laid before them. "Gosh, it's beautiful," says the man, for lack of more descriptive words. "Folks told me so who've been here, but it's more than they said."

Up, up the road goes between towering snowdrifts. To the west we gaze across to the Cascades. Closer by, two peaks emblazoned white command our amazement. Beyond them lies gigantic, lumbering Mount McLoughlin, and at the horizon's far reaches (about 150 miles into California) the vague white outline of Mount Shasta (14,162 feet). Easterly lies Mount Scott; southerly a great sweep of evergreen forest stretches to the limit of sight. The place is humbling, mysterious, ethereal, like gazing into the starry wonder of the night sky. Feeling this remarkable spot, marveling at it, absorbing its gestalt, we want to retain it for the rest of our lives because we realize no photograph we have taken, no combination of words I may write will simulate our experience here.

At both Rainier and Crater Lake we have been fortunate in having phenomenal weather. The brisk, dry, sun-soaked clarity of the air permits spectacularly crisp views. We applaud ourselves on our good luck; the world is smiling again.

The north road plunges swiftly from Crater Lake to a lower valley albeit still high altitude. Quickly we are in Fort Klamath and stop for a coffee break in a clean, friendly, storefront restaurant with 1920s-vintage plain wide oak tables and straight-back chairs. Two middle-aged women in print dresses run the place. No chance of finding a restaurant chain out here. From a limited menu we settle for apple cobbler and coffee, with no regrets.

As we follow U.S. 97 across a flat valley floor, Mount McLoughlin, a perfect snow laden cone, juts up on our right. The highway embraces the shore of the thirty mile long Upper Klamath Lake, the largest natural fresh water lake west of the Mississippi. Shasta peeks between distant hills. The scene is wide. Black pelicans stand motionless on rocks in the water, their wings outspread, drying.

"At least they look like pelicans," I say. "Fresh water variety, I suppose. Seen them only in Florida or on the West Coast. Oops, a sign. We're passing through Pelican City. They must be pelicans. What do you know!"

Speaking of pelicans, Danny brings up President Reagan, although I fail to understand the association—not that it matters.

"He's got lots of guts, resolve, charisma, but no brains. The presidency is only another acting role—Rap Master Ronnie."

"You may be right. But he's a wonder for a man his

age. I admire his energy and determination."

A journal comment: Reagan gives me and perhaps others my age hope that our own physical and mental powers have time to run. For our sake, don't screw up, Ronnie; don't disenchant the younger generations. It's tough enough having to put up with America's worship of youth.

South of Klamath Falls, Shasta constantly beckons— a massive white cone dominating the landscape at every glimpse from every direction, the left and the right, from straight ahead, depending on the turns of the road. Sixty miles away it is majestic; a few miles away, overpowering. The north face is virtually covered with snow. A cloud puff, the only cloud in the entire blue expanse, floats like a parasol above Shasta's summit. High, forested hills guard the perimeter of its outer base. Small valleys lie tucked between the hills. In the valleys cattle graze in golden fields of parched grass.

A marsh, a place called Grass Lake Rest Area, lies among ponderosas in the hills below Shasta. The tablet at Grass Lake explains that Shasta rises 3,500 feet higher above its base than Rainier; hence it appears more grandiose.

Grass Lake was the victim of human folly. Early in the century a thirty-two room hotel stood on its shore until someone set off dynamite below the lake surface, draining it like a suddenly unplugged bathtub, and leaving the hotel at the edge of a large tract of soggy ground. However, it turned out the loss to humans has been a gain to wildlife. The marsh is now a friendly habitat to both water and land creatures and the only place in the world where the ten-inch tiger salamander exists. None showed themselves during our visit. An appealing and refreshing spot, we find it just right for lunch (of chicken rice soup and nuts).

A motorist in a business suit, also resting at Grass Lake, tells us that south on U.S. 97 as he passed Redding the temperature was 97 degrees, with 107 predicted for the Sacramento Valley this afternoon (just where we are heading), as well as for the next three days

"But our pickup is air-conditioned, right Danny? Oh, yes, literally, simply by opening windows. So we'll let it all come in, just let it all come in."

When I first saw Shasta a couple of years ago on a trip with Jane, I was less impressed than I am now. But my second visit to the Delaware Water Gap was disappointing. What is there about Shasta? About the moment? About myself? Am I now freer than when I was here before, freer than when the trip began? Am I now in closer touch with the universe?

The northern approach to Shasta on Route 97 is breathtaking. The road circling the foot of the mountain affords a clean, untrammeled, total view of its immensity from base to summit. It is a spectacle of earth mass, of sheer bulk, miniaturizing all else: hills, trees, the pickup, ourselves. Not to derogate Rainier's grandeur, we passed no point from which an unobstructed show of that mountain in its entirety was possible. But at Shasta only an open desert lies between us and the entire gigantic cone.

At an intersection in Weed crowded with service stations, we stop for gas. A middle-aged male attendant leaves the pump running unattended at our tank. When he returns long after it has shut itself off, I ask him to wash our insect-spattered windshield.

"Do it yourself," he says, indignantly. "You're in California now, buddy."

"Asshole," Danny exclaims as we drive away. "No

wonder there's a net outflow of people from California these days."

"Who could feel welcome here?" I assent.

From I-5 the west face of Shasta is worn and rougher but still "a wow of a sight to see" as Danny put it.

At Castella on the wide, smooth, broadly curving superhighway, we barrel gradually down, down, down, to a hotter, hotter, ever hotter clime.

"It's a hot time in the valley this afternoon, I'll say, Danny."

Emerging from the last of the mountains, I look back longingly for a final sight of Shasta. Mount Lassen floats in the distant left. The hot, wide, flat valley is monotonous, anticlimactic after the thrills of Crater Lake and Shasta. Hour after hour, mile after mile, I-5 slices through a flat, sizzling green world of irrigated crops and grazing cattle to Sacramento. The pickup cab is an oven. Over Corning, just ahead, streaks of smog hang in the dead air. Soaked with sweat, my undershirt is glued to the back of the seat. Only the rush of air by the open windows and the quiet drone of the engine is heard. The sky is hazy blue, the land green with endless orchards.

The interstate is ideal for driving the boring miles. Near Bayliss, its four lanes are double barreled and bullet straight, its center strip lushly covered for miles with a low wall of blooming red, pink and white oleander. Under the circumstances, I-5 gets us efficiently and not unpleasantly to our destination. Danny's estimated time of arrival in Sacramento, about which he was so positive back in Redding, is off by two hours. How could he make such a whopping error? It shakes my confidence in his judgment.

"How are you doing?" asks Danny at the wheel.

"In this heat? I'm having a great sauna bath."

"Well, at least it's free."

With reception from a public radio station faint, we listen to an orchestra playing Tchaikovsky's Romeo and Juliet Overture that lulls us into a long introspective silence.

Suddenly Danny says, "Yesterday I felt lonely because I didn't have a girl." I censor my reaction, the thought that despite being married, I've been lonely for years.

Instead I ask, "Isn't loneliness a feeling of emptiness deep within that yearns for giving and receiving love?"

The KOA in West Sacramento is the priciest yet: fourteen dollars a night. It is the most crowded and has the poorest facilities, but what the hell, we decide to put up with it. After all, we're here only to visit Carl and his family in Davis.

They are hospitable hosts, apologetic for not offering us their home for the night, especially since Jane and I had shared ours with them twice on their visits to Cape Cod. Of course I understand they have no choice. They have visitors from England and their son Frank is home from college. No need to apologize, I assure them again and again. Frank, Danny's contemporary, always looked up to Danny. Sam, living at home, a year or two younger than Frank, is gentle, sweet tempered, and slightly retarded.

We are greeted with smiling embraces and kisses. After an introduction to the couple from England, we sit together chatting and sipping wine in the living room. Not having been with friends since Chicago, I feel warm and comfortable among familiar, welcoming faces. And I'm surprised at how isolated I have felt despite Danny's company. Slender, red faced, curly haired Frank soon shows up with his pretty sloe-eyed girlfriend.

The English couple, fiftyish, visiting professors, are cool, correct, and cautious. They never genuinely warm up during the hours of our visit. Among the nine of us, conversation switches back and forth throughout the evening, so that eventually everyone learns something new about everyone else. With drinks in hand, we step to the patio in the garden, where Carl tends a bed of hot coals. The English couple mention their country's continuing brain drain. They are amazed at our flowers and are shocked at the terrible clear-cutting of forests on their tour of Washington state. With restrained pride, they talk about their teen-age children back home.

Leaving the patio we merge again at the dining table and feast on Irene's barbecued lamb and salad, potatoes, and later desserts. The dinner is superb, the best on our journey. She and Carl tell of their plans for a month-long trip to New Zealand and Australia with the boys. Since Carl is a scientist renown in his field and much in demand, they travel the world.

Danny talks of his travels, especially his most recent, to Japan. Coveting Danny's freedom and worldly experience, Frank listens intently.

By ten, warmed by hours of friendship, content and sleepy from the wine and the good home-cooked meal, Danny and I reluctantly depart. Otherwise we'll end up on the floor. The family accompanies us to their driveway and sees us off with crushing hugs, smiles and entreaties to return. Pangs of sadness rise within me the minute I slam shut the door of the pickup.

"They make you feel like a member of the family," says Danny.

"Yes, and don't they have a wonderful closeness among themselves?" I say, knowing that he misses such an intimacy in our own family. Or am I projecting my own emptiness and sense of failure? No, the contrast between our families is glaring. They are visibly cohesive; we are in a process of disintegration.

I recount the story of how Carl and Irene met.

"Remember the Kincaid apartment at the corner of Kimbark in Chicago? Well, Carl was living there too, working on his Ph.D. Irene was the older sister of the one who died of multiple sclerosis. I had no inkling of any romance between Carl and Irene then. Years later, perhaps twenty, I learned that he and Irene were married and raising a family."

"It's remarkable how you could just pick up where you left off," says Danny, intrigued that a friendship has lasted so long, and that a friendship that was once only casual, can, after years, turn into something warm and secure.

"I suspect we have a common bond in our children," I explain. "Which of course was not the case when we were students."

If this is so, what will happen to the friendship if we are no longer an integrated family? I ask myself. No, no, I couldn't bear such a loss, of my family, of such friends.

On the drive back to the KOA Danny claims to have detected a certain frustration in Frank, a reluctance to break away despite an urge to do so. He has decided on a course to follow, chosen a career, yet somehow you get the feeling he has compromised himself.

"The trouble is there's no adventure in his life. No uncertainty."

In Danny's world a surfeit of both surely exists. The two young men are a fascinating contrast: the one stable, secure, surrounded by love, following a sure, unexciting path, the other, unsure, lonely, searching for inner peace, criss-crossing the earth to escape from himself. Sensing Danny's envy when Frank first entered the room with his girl friend, I felt great empathy for him. Each lad needs only a little of what the other has, but wants it all.

As soon as we arrive at the KOA, I phone Jane. Friends have been taking her out to dinner, to the movies, to an opera, and she's been busy teaching painting, has five students now. Were it wintertime, she'd be lonely, but this season with so many friends summering on the Cape, she's hardly ever alone.

"Our son is suffering, Jane, and it pains me to see him like this."

"I know," she says. "How are the two of you getting along?"

"Ninety percent of the time okay," I reply. "Our differences are not earthshaking; our care for each other is the important thing." Talking about our son saves us from having to talk about what's most on our minds, our troubled marriage.

I'm suddenly in a foul mood. The damned temperature reached 105 today. Only the truck motor remained cool. Tonight the miserable KOA campsites are jammed, the sinks and toilets are a mess of paper wads, and goddamn snoring reverberates through the grounds. Lying dripping naked in the dark in the heat that's locked into the truck, we talk before falling off to sleep.

"Your mother's not lonely, and I'm not either; I have you. Are you lonely?"

"Sometimes."

"Even with me?"

"Yes, even with you."

How very, very sad, I think.

"Now sleep, that's all that matters, let's sleep."

In the middle of the night a crying child awakens me. I'm sleeping lightly these past nights, not typical of the way it's been.

DAY THIRTEEN
Lake Tahoe & Yosemite

I hear the first moaning of traffic at 5:00 a.m. as I lay lazily awake thinking of how much I dislike cities, especially their sounds. Cities, the ultimate in pollution—noise, air, water—and slummy sights. Only in architecture and culture are cities redeeming, but my enjoyment of these features is not enough to compensate for their abhorrent artificiality. I am eager to break away and tour the magnificent California countryside.

The superhighway I-80 to Reno leads also to Lake Tahoe and Yosemite. The morning radio predicts a heat wave for the next three days in the valley—not the place to be. *We'll* certainly not be there. Mountains, here we come. Yippee.

I mull over again our canceled visit with cousins in San Rafael. They are young, hard working, putting in long hours. Have I alienated them? Have I placed convenience ahead of our relationship?

Breakfast at a truck stop is the best, the most perfect meal of the day. In our family, Danny and I alone share the pleasure of having big breakfasts. His mother and both sisters have no appetite in the morning.

The interstate takes high-altitude Donner Pass, a place where winters are hard. But today the calm, bracing air smells of pines and sweet vegetation. Having read the fascinating story of the Donner party as a boy, I now describe briefly to Danny their tragedy in the deep snow, of the cannibalism that occurred at this very place, and of a survivor's bragging of having eaten the tender flesh of children.

We reach the summit at 7,227 feet. Donner Lake nestles below in a valley. Around us snow softens the high ridges etched into the vivid sky. Right along Route 89, the road to Tahoe, fly-fishermen are snapping their lines into the Truckee River that runs boisterously beside the road.

All Danny and I know of fly-fishing derives from *A River Runs Through It*, the book I gave him in Montana and which he's halfway through. Maclean depicts fly-fishing as a lesson in the art of living. Treasuring Maclean's book, I regret not getting to know him better when I was his student. How little we actually know each other, how much we miss seeing, understanding, appreciating. How much I missed seeing in Danny until now.

He is impatient with a driver ahead hesitating to pass a slow moving truck. Quite spontaneously the subject of our arguments comes up. Danny wishes for more harmony between us.

"Nothing wrong with having differences," I say. "You don't take things lying down. You stick by your guns—a good quality."

Can he in some way see himself positively?

"I guess I'm really aggressive," he says, "in a quiet way." Not so quiet as he thinks, I muse to myself.

Elevation 6,200 feet, Lake Tahoe is a disappointment, hardly the pristine, preserved, natural playground I gleaned from movies. At Tahoe City large sailboats lie at unruffled moorings. The town's main street teems with banks, small shops, rest homes, condos, a medical building, dentist offices, a chiropractor whose parking lot is full.

The lake's shoreline is fouled by homes crammed one on the other; some are elaborate and expensively stone faced, screaming their presence, monuments to affluence and ego. The shoreland between the road and the northwest corner of the lake is only one house deep, negating privacy. Bordering the lake closely at other spots, the road encroaches on the natural beauty of the perimeter.

Shortly after Kings Beach, another busy, crowded resort town, we cross the Nevada line at Crystal Bay. Suddenly here are gambling casinos—Thunder Rose, for example—and large resort hotels. The Hyatt is of city proportions. Private homes hang off steep cliffs rising from the shore. A wall of high-rise condos cuts off the view of the water. Nevada boasts yet more new, huge, ostentatious, bewildering megahomes. Seeing a large swimming pool beside the sandy beach of the lake, I fail to see the need for it.

"The lake's too cold for comfortable swimming," Danny explains.

The northeastern Nevada side of the lake is a state park, undeveloped save for the paved road itself. Last winter's snow poles still mark both road shoulders. An occasional deer browses by the roadside. A tall pine forest blankets the cliffs that drop sharply to the shore.

The day is sparkling and comfortable with low humidity. After yesterday's valley heat, we feel fortunate to be here. From across the lake a snowcapped mountain range provides a gorgeous backdrop to the lake's southern edge. One of the mountains, Monument Peak, soars 10,000 feet. But a large sight-seeing boat on the lake suddenly ruptures the purity of the scene.

The shopping center in South Lake Tahoe is tastefully done, but the rest fails to impress me. High-rise hotels, casinos, and an all-glass office building comprise the hub of downtown. The casinos bear names such as Flesh'n Fantasy, Hannah's, and Caesar's. Harvey's has a sign announcing a performance by Neil Sedaka. The main street traffic moves like an army of ants.

Did I know that South Lake Tahoe is two towns? Danny asks. The Nevada side is a mini-Las Vegas; the California side, where gambling is illegal, consists mainly of a long string of garish motels. The California town is like a bag lady; the Nevada town like a blonde bombshell. But the two towns are truly symbiotic; neither can prosper without the other.

Stopping at a restaurant for coffee, we encounter a line of people waiting to be served and decide not to wait. South Lake Tahoe is a typical, crowded American resort with too many cars, restaurants, and motels, too many people, too much of everything, period. In front of a tiered parking lot, plantings are struggling to survive. This place is definitely not for us, we agree. It's only for birds and fools. Let's get out of here, now.

This July on Route 207 there's still snow on the heights above Tahoe. From the summit we gaze over a broad green valley that lies between mountain ranges, repeating the basin and range geologic pattern of the Far West. Homes and condos interrupt the forest, tarnishing the landscape. Carved into the mountainside, the road weaves downward in a spectacular series of reverse curves, which fails to impress us after the sights we've already seen. Has our trip passed its scenic climax? Are we now inured to nature's spectacle?

From our vantage point on U.S. 395 in the valley, Route 207 behind us shows as an obvious slice through the mountains. We can see more clearly from here that the condos we had passed are perched on the tops of ridges and stare out at the emptiness. On this, the east side of the high Sierra, the mountains are dry, chaparral covered almost to their peaks, which, being cooler, are lightly forested with conifers. Warm though this valley is, it never reaches the ovenlike temperatures of the Sacramento Valley on the westerly side of the Sierra.

In Minden, a clean, attractive town of one-story buildings, we have a nutritious, solid lunch at Maddy's, a surprisingly sophisticated restaurant for so remote a place. Refreshed, we speed down the hot, dry valley floor, a slot between hot, dry mountain ranges. Distant slopes and peaks to the west are snow laden. Topaz Lake, entirely surrounded by round, low, barren hills, spreads before us to the east.

We cross the Sweetwater range at 6,000 feet. Near the road the white-water rapids of the Sweetwater River rush down a steeply graded, rock-strewn stream bed. Ahead are snowy Eagle Peak and Hanna Mountain at 11,800 feet. We cross Devil's Gate Pass at 7,519 feet, and enter a haunting, barren, high valley of faded green chaparral. The quiet valley meanders among low beige-green hills, bewitching in their spareness.

Near Bridgeport the land on our right extends flat green to snowy mountains; on our left an azure lake in barren land. Cattle are grazing by the road. Ahead are 12,000-foot black-and-white-streaked daggers stabbing the empty sky. As if we were oddly suspended in space, smooth waves of low hills, here and there a colony of trees, trail off to the rounded, glistening white summits of the high Sierra.

What could possibly surpass the great natural beauty we have seen? But it's a foolish question. Is one flower more beautiful than another? What makes the world so beautiful?

What above all else have I found most satisfying on this journey? Variety, variety—each valley, each mountain, each day, each hour, each creature, each human being, unique. The trip across this incredible land is my finest teacher.

Rolling down switchbacks from 8,000 feet, we stop at a view point to digest the great panorama of salty Mono Lake spread before us. Rough peaks pierce the crisp horizon like shards of steel. Then the road takes us close by the lake, a wide blue bowl reflecting a blue heaven full of floating marshmallow-shaped puffs.

Route 120 leads to the dramatic north entrance of Yosemite. We stare up at a giant, bare, rocky, snow-spattered ridge, feeling tiny. Hewn from the rock walls of bare peaks, Route 120 is but a slender tier snaking above a deep, narrow rock valley. The slabbed slopes are a madness of crags, scoured by glaciers, eroded by the elements. A sign indicates 9,000 feet; small, dark blue Ellery Lake to our left is at 9,513 feet. Snow-tipped rock stilettos rise 2,000 feet above us.

Tioga Pass, the highest point at 9,945 feet, is a wilderness of unimaginable, towering, smooth granite domes. The unsullied sky is brittle blue; an army of clean white clouds parades from the west. The landscape is vast—sheets of rock on all sides; sheer mountain flanks of smooth, polished rock; solid, dense, hostile rock—a landscape on a scale of its own. Yet in the granite crannies blue and pink flowers, even small pines, find a home.

Although our gas tank wasn't full before entering Yosemite, an unnecessary risk, Danny assures me that we have plenty of fuel to traverse the park. Keeping quiet, I am uneasy. Danny's assurances haven't always been reliable, such as his miscalculation of our arrival time in Sacramento.

He doesn't realize that things rarely go according to plan. He doesn't understand that it's wise to always hedge one's bets.

My conception of Yosemite Valley was based on Ansel Adams's photos and the nineteenth-century paintings of Thomas Moran. It seemed to me a place of great wonder and untrammeled beauty. But on this day that notion is marred.

The valley road follows a strong, full river of rushing green rapids. Tourists in rubber rafts float by in the current. Since many students are on summer break, families flock to the park. Among such crowds, hundreds of tents, cooking grills, vans, and cars, all serenity is erased. I am despondent. To top it off, gasoline in the park sells for an absurd $1.36/ gallon.

A 3,000 foot vertical glazed granite slab, El Capitan, shoots up from the level verdant floor. The glossy green, foam-streaked Merced River slithers by the rock's base. As we study the astonishing escarpment, Danny comments that many have climbed the sheer face, to my mind an impossible feat. We drive by another great upright slab, Half Dome.

Yosemite Falls drops 2,500 feet in two stages. From a precipitous granite cliff, a narrow white ribbon tumbles gracefully, almost in slow motion, gradually widening into a diaphanous plume. After plunging with a roar from its second stage into a pool, it bathes the surrounding air with a fine mist. Fed by the constant moisture, rich green vegetation blankets every inch of surrounding earth.

The falls is a marvel of creation, similar to a thundering ocean surf. Both natural phenomena are humbling to witness. With the falls as background, we take pictures of each other, proof that we are here. Although it's hard to break the spell of the falls and simply walk away, we resist lingering. We view what we came to see, but more sights remain. We drive on to other sections of the park.

From Glacier Point and Washburn Point we get a sure feel for the history of our planet's dramatic upheaval. Sculpted granite mountains rim the horizon in all directions. In the near distance across a wide chasm, a double waterfall rumbles faintly: Nevada Falls, not as high as, but issuing greater volume than, Yosemite Falls.

No photograph can replicate the enormous magnitude of the scene, still, we try. From our height Yosemite Falls is in the shade, too dark for a shot. After taking several "breathtaking" shots, I realize I've forgotten to remove the camera lens cover. So life is full of lost opportunities. We see birds gliding below us, yes *below* us, in the transparent depth of Yosemite Valley, where we had been a half hour before. But we've had enough of the noisy, boisterous crowds who jam the viewing sites. The aura of quieter days is over, sadly obliterated by the throng. Beauty and serenity are undemocratic.

"It's too bad there's a road to Glacier Point," Danny says. "To earn such a reward we should have to work for it and hike there on foot."

I concur.

Unlike our gradual approach to the spectacular Tioga Pass entrance from the north, the road south through the park follows a steeper, seemingly interminable grade down to Route 41 and Fish Camp, Oakhurst, Coarsegold, and Fresno. A coyote lopes unafraid for a time alongside our truck. We rattle down, down, down, curve, reverse curve, curve, reverse curve, mile after mile. A sweet fragrance pervades the cab.

"The fragrance is from the Zaneta bush, I think," says

Danny. "I've smelled it in the desert."

Tense, I'm flooring the mat with both feet. "You're going too fast, Danny."

"Don't worry. I'm in perfect control."

"Maybe you are, but for my sake slow down. Maybe I've got a hangup about this; please respect it. Okay?"

"Okay, Dad, Okay."

The southern entrance to Yosemite is dense evergreen forest, part of the Sierra National Forest, which blankets the western side of the mountains. Under the influence still of the magnificent natural sights we have just seen, the man-made world of Oakhurst seems ordinary, dull, false. But we adjust in an instant, accept the loss of beauty, and take a comfortable air-conditioned motel room, (as we descended from the mountains the temperature rose). We have a delicious dinner at the Old Barn, with its friendly atmosphere, and enjoy a cheerful evening together, my son and I.

Overhearing us talk of Yosemite's glories, our cordial young waitress confesses that she hasn't been in the park for two years or more.

She shrugs. "I don't know why, because I always find it very pretty. I suppose life's responsibilities have taken over."

I'm amused at her use of "very pretty," clearly the descriptive understatement of our trip.

After phoning Jane's Uncle Morris in Santa Monica, my final destination, I realize with bittersweet feelings that we have only one day left, a day less than planned. To avoid the heavy holiday traffic, Uncle Morris suggests we not spend Friday, July 4, on the highway.

"Try to be here for Thursday night," he urges.

"I'll call to let you know how we're doing," I promise.

As Danny and I clink our glasses of wine, toasting a mostly satisfying journey, I tell him, "Thanks for being so patient with me." With the trip winding down, I try to sum up in my mind what our experience together has done for us. We have achieved a deeper understanding of each other, a greater respect and a fuller appreciation of each other. We've destroyed a lot of barriers. I have a good feeling about us.

Soothed by the wine, Danny again talks of his trip east with Pam, reiterating, with some regret, that he hadn't consummated his relationship with her. I tell him how much I admire his continence, his consideration for her. He notes the attractiveness of several women diners near us, as has been his frequent habit on other occasions in public places. Our conversation is a repetition of the one we had in Essex, Connecticut, on our first day of the trip, an eternity ago.

"I can't share your interest," I say, repeating what I said that day. "I no longer dream about what I can't have. Nor do I have the desire. Anyway I hope you realize outward appearance is a very thin basis for a relationship."

Danny agrees, and tells of a skiing adventure with a beautiful but bitchy girl who told him she hated her father.

"Even though she was terrific to look at, after I got to know her I couldn't wait to dump her," he says. "She was all screwed up. But I can't help it. My gonads keep working like hell."

"I know, Danny. The words in the song go 'Like a runaway truck, I just gotta fuck.' Tomorrow on the road to Fresno, we'll play John Fogerty's *I Can't Help Myself.* We are like Yosemite, products of a great, relentless natural process."

Knowing how helpless Danny is, I am just as helpless to ease his persistent, overwhelming unhappiness. I have taken on his pain.

DAY FOURTEEN
California

Both of us slept well in the motel room last night. I dreamed that Jane's married cousin Fanny, an expressive, independent type, was visiting us on Cape Cod with a group of young people—her brood perhaps. We left the house together to go shopping in a skyscraper in the city. The dream strikes me as full of foreboding, of a desire to be free.

Danny and I have a cheery and relaxed breakfast in a busy informal Oakhurst restaurant. The conversation is wide ranging, including a discussion on my progressive baldness, ongoing since I was twenty-one. Danny speculates on whether he has inherited the gene although he has yet to see any sign of its influence.

Inexplicably, I mention my perverse grandmother on my mother's side. She had four husbands. I worshipped the second one as my grandfather although we weren't blood related. A saintly man, Lincolnesque and lanky, with a bass voice, Sam owned a small hot-dog and hamburger hole-in-the-wall at the Fanueil Hall marketplace in Boston before it was renovated to its present antiseptic condition as Quincy Market. In those days the locale hummed with the comings and goings of farmers unloading their produce.

Everyone loved Sam for his good nature, and delighted in the picturesque foot-high white chef's hat perched on his head while working. He was my boyhood model, a colorful, gentle, generous man, secretly slipping me a quarter at every visit. I was seventeen when he died painfully of stomach cancer, my first loss of someone I loved, my first inkling that life is often cruel. That image of my last hospital visit to see him is still vivid after so many years.

In my ruminations, I recall Uncle Bill, my grandmother's brother, an intermittent millionaire and pauper, once owner of a hotel, a racetrack, an amusement park, and a playhouse. With most of his wealth depleted at the time of his death in his seventies, he was reduced to operating a rundown restaurant and bar in Fitchburg.

In his better days, back in the thirties when most people were poor, he and his second wife, Tiabe, traveled about in a spic-and-span, mile-long, chauffeur driven Oldsmobile. I marveled that Uncle Bill could blithely ignore the chauffeur waiting outside patiently by the automobile while he visited. Once, on a rare visit to our home, learning that it was my tenth birthday, he reached into his small vest pocket, withdrew a gold Waltham pocket watch with roman numerals on its face, disengaged it from a gold chain, and handed it to me—my birthday present. I was, and to this day still am, overwhelmed. Some events last forever.

On that same birthday my parents gave me what I then wanted most, a dictionary. It was cheaply bound, poorly printed, and incomplete—a disappointment—although I never let on. Is that what they thought of me? Uncle Bill thought I was worth a gold watch. Years later I realized that was the most my parents could afford during the depression. I should have been told that. Our personalities are molded by erroneous interpretations of experience.

I tell Danny of my only sibling, a younger brother, whose bluster hides an interior sensitivity and keen intelligence, which Jane refuses to see.

"How intolerant we can be and ignorant of each other's interior life. Why do we forget that it exists? Our actions, our behavior aren't as obvious as we think."

Another scorcher today. As early as 8:00 a.m. an oppressive heat overlays the valley like a transparent veil. The earth is dry, yellow, sere. Only the trees, their long branches extended, are green. The road burrows through an irrigated orchard of thousands of fruit trees. Fresno radio predicts a high of 102 degrees; it is 84 at 9:30. Zipping along at sixty-five, Danny beats the steering wheel with both hands to the rhythm of rock music. He loses himself in the blasting sound. Somehow he is alien and I become frightened.

"Take it easy," I shout. "Slow down."

"They're playing my rock music," he says. "It's passé now but they keep playing it for us baby boomers because we're still the largest listening group."

"Interesting," I say. "I like some of your songs, but why so loud?"

"I still can't get over that you like them."

Farther on the way toward Kings Canyon, Winkler, and Squaw Valley, a thick, hot haze envelops the low, bare hills. Kings River runs full, strong, and glassy beside the road for a while. Soon we are speeding alongside the concrete-lined Frank Kern Canal amid immense fruit groves and grape arbors, with small irrigation ditches gurgling between the rows. Tremendous trucks, loaded high with giant spruce logs, grind by, a common sight throughout the West, especially in eastern California.

Up, up the road goes towards Kings Canyon to a height overlooking a patchwork of valley hills of dark green trees scattered across an orange grassland. Fresno radio now predicts cooler temperatures for tomorrow, down to 97 degrees.

"Yea! yea!," we scream. "A 97-degree cold wave."

Is that crested bird running across the road a roadrunner? Could be, could be, speculates Danny, who has seen them before here and there.

At 4,000 feet we are in pines again, comfortably cooler and looking down at low, rounded hills. More timber trucks from the mountains pass us. One particular behemoth carries only two logs, so enormous are they. At 5,000 feet the valley below disappears under a blanket of hot, brown haze. A sign by the road reads: "Sequoia National Forest— Land of Many Uses."

"Especially logging," I remark.

"Reagan's a jerk," says Danny angrily, referring to our president's pro-business, anti-conservationist policy.

Kings Canyon is dry, high desert country. From the ridge, Kings River appears as a white-flecked green sliver on the bottom of a deep pale brown canyon. The rocky land is rough and raw, wildly beautiful, without Yosemite's smooth polished surfaces. Snow glistens on faraway mountains.

We become exasperated looking for a parking place at the park's entrance.

"This place is too accessible," I say. "Isn't it our way—the American way—to make it convenient and easy?"

Finally we find a spot and park the truck. Following the signs on foot, we first visit the General Grant tree, a forty foot circumference sequoia, then the smaller General Lee tree.

"Only a lousy thirty-six feet," says Danny.

Taking a narrow, bumpy, dirt road to Panorama Point, Danny impatiently tails a slow van in front of us. He'd hate having someone doing it to him, I think, annoyed.

We park in a small clearing carpeted with pine needles.

A trail, cushiony underfoot, takes us to the Point through a tall, calm, sweetly fragrant wood of hemlock and spruce. The view at the point is a variation on Yosemite, extending thirty-two miles to 14,000-foot mountain peaks, and no less breathtaking.

Returning to the crowded visitor center and restaurant, we have a relaxed talk over lunch of when, at age thirty, I joined my father in his small custom upholstering business. Wishing to retire and promising me a free hand, he persuaded me to leave a girl and a good job in Chicago to take over his enterprise. It was a powerful offer. Having my own business had been a long-held dream. And I persuaded my brother, an interior decorator, to join me in what I thought would be a winning combination.

However, it turned out that my father, having no intention of bowing out, instead retained final authority, especially in matters of dispensing funds. A frightened product of the Depression, he kept expenses down to the bare bones, and refused to run any risks. Ready to sell my car and pour my small savings into the business, I was unable to convince my brother to do the same. His wife was outraged by my suggestion. In a few months, sick of my father's interference and conservatism, I left to take a job in Rhode Island. My brother soon departed as well. Years later, my mother confessed that their proposition had been a ruse to induce me away from my Catholic girlfriend in Chicago.

Danny listens quietly without comment, no doubt having heard the story before in bits and pieces.

"One good feature about being retired: I can now afford the luxury of having friends strictly for friendship's sake, not for economic gain. Being friends in business is never pure. No matter what we think, we can't be sure of our motives. How can we be?"

A small, friendly brook, its banks dense with red, pink, blue, and white wildflowers, runs beside the road to Sequoia National Park. At Lost Grove, we take a cool walk beneath the sequoias, tender giants with their thick, relatively short arms covered with delicate green bristles.

The pass is at 7,300 feet. Why my sudden fear of heights?

"Maybe it's because of your age," Danny offers.

"My age?"

"Yeah, being old, closer to the time you'll die."

It's true, death is nearer. Do I value life more now? Makes sense, but I keep quiet.

On the road again, we glimpse a beautiful, peaceful meadow scooped out of the forest. From the main parking lot at Sequoia, it's a short walk to what is billed as "the largest growing thing", the General Sherman tree. With the tree as background, we take pictures of each other. When I show the snapshots back home, I imagine saying, This is Danny and the "thing," me and the falls, Danny and the mountain, me and a new friend at Glacier.

Most sequoias have been burned some time in their four-figure lives. Evidence of old fires abound. Part of a natural process, it is the fire of life. New trees grow from the char and thrive. Violent death renders a good. Will Danny's pain and suffering come to any good? Must we too burn to grow?

Naming the giants after generals is fitting; famous generals are also giants. Of course the greatest is aptly named for Sherman, considered mad by intimates, whose cruel march through Georgia is infamous. Lee, a noble loser, and Grant, an irresponsible drunk, obviously rate only third and second largest respectively.

Being in Sequoia is dwarfing. It also provokes philosophical speculation. A man's T-shirt seen at the General Sherman tree observes: "Life's a bitch. Marry one and then you die."

"Isn't that what I was saying last night?" says Danny.

Inspired, I compose my own profound bumper sticker aphorism: "Being dwarfed is great fun." Danny laughs in snide appreciation.

Moro Rock, a massive protrusion jutting from a 6,700-foot cliff, overlooks an immense canyon 4,000 feet deep. Danny lights a cigarette as we mount a stairway carved in the rock and head into the blue. What a fool, I think; he's deliberately killing himself. He races ahead of me without stopping while I rest now and then.

The view from Moro's summit rivals Yosemite and Panorama Point in dramatic vastness. There's no limit to the surprises.

"California is the most beautiful place of all," I say. Danny smiles and nods, for this has been his show.

Too fascinated to leave, we linger by a pipe rail while new visitors arrive. Many speak foreign languages. They come to see America, and boy, what a show we give.

The southern road down from Sequoia is the steepest yet. Zigzag turns pile one upon the other astride sheer vertical drops. The dizzy ride spirals on and on as we drop and drop and drop. Moro Rock arches above us. About two-thirds of the way down the grade a sign announces: "Hill."

"Really? No kidding. Who'da thunk it?"

Nearing the high valley bottom, we pass a 12-to-15-foot-tall yucca plant by the roadside, the largest I've ever seen. It's hot now even at 2,000 feet.

"God help us in the big valley."

A river runs white along the valley floor. Dry, scrubby hills surround Lake Kaweah, an inviting blue expanse formed by a dam at its western end. Near the dam is a dark green orchard, restful to our eyes against the parched, yellow hills.

Ahead are Visalia, Lemoncove, and Three Rivers. Back in a sauna again; we pause for lemonade at a fast-food restaurant in Vasalia; the thermometer reads 101 degrees at 5:00 p.m.

"Wow!" we say together.

"I'm sorry, Dad. I promised you Mount Whitney from Moro Rock," Danny says, having several times assured me it was visible from there.

"That's OK, Danny. I'm impressed enough." He's trying hard to please, too hard, perhaps. He wanted me to see Mount Whitney but he didn't realize it was more than he could deliver and is disappointed in himself.

His attention suddenly turns to admiring the girls in the fast-food place. I feel sorry for him.

Red, pink, and white flowers on the tall full oleander bushes shield the cars in oncoming lanes. Flowers brighten both sides of Route 99 at Tulare. I read on the side of a passing beer truck: "In passing may we suggest Muller's Blue Ribbon Beer?" Signs tell us we are near Earlimart, Ducor, and Terra Bella. A long train of tank cars dogs us on the strip that separates the road from the orchards and orange groves, which seem to extend into the flat forever. A hot wind blows under an empty blue heaven. We are a half hour from Bakersfield and dinner in a cool place.

The cruise control doesn't work. It hasn't worked on

the entire trip because Danny failed to have it fixed before we left. At the beginning I was annoyed, but now I'm used to being without it. Furthermore I've let up on him. He's not had an easy time. In the motel last night he was awakened by the itching of old mosquito bites. He still bears welts from two nights ago in West Sacramento. I feel for him.

We listen to *All Things Considered* on PBS before entering Bakersfield. The station fades. On another we find a lovely Salieri flute concerto, somehow refreshing in the heat. It's a pity to switch it off as we veer into the parking lot of Stuart Anderson's American Grill.

The restaurant's decor is pleasing, the food excellent, the air cool. Our waitress is a friendly young woman named Leatha, according to a small tag on her uniform.

"It's pronounced Leetha," she explains with enthusiasm.

"What a strange and beautiful name," I exclaim.

"I'm named after my dad's old girlfriend."

"You mean your dad named you but your mother didn't know where he got the name?" I ask intrigued.

"She didn't know until ten years after," she bubbled.

"I'll bet she was sore."

"They're divorced."

"I don't wonder."

"Dad's a maintenance man for a big retail chain. He just loves working the acre of land he owns in Bakersfield. Used to be a Missouri farmer. Is this your son?"

"Yup. We've just crossed the country together." I give her a quick rundown of what we've seen.

"Gosh, that's terrific. I wish I knew my dad when he was a boy. I'd have loved to be his friend."

After dinner I am strongly aware that our trip is

almost at its close. A Mozart sonata for piano and violin is now playing on the truck radio. After good wine, a friendly waitress, full stomach, and great music, the drive down the smooth highway is a pleasure, despite the early evening heat. Danny and I are at peace with each other. Our journey is ending on a sweet note—musically as well as comradely.

The strains of Schubert now flood the cab. The sun, lowering in the northwest, brightens our way from behind us. We are converging on the Tehachapi Mountains, purple shadows in the near distance. The warm wind is growing cooler. The cultivated land is like a great green pool table lying between a mountain range to our left and another to our right.

We are conscious of traveling through time as well as space as daylight fades. The eveningfall is beautiful and soft. The sound of the engine is a smooth drone. In the waning light the mountains assume a muted orange. Streaks of brown smog float in the middle air to our left. The mountains now seem artificial in the haze, like a stage set backdrop. A variety of sweet unidentifiable fragrances pervades the air. The setting sun, the warm air, the gentle tones, sounds, and colors, form a mellow ambiance. Nearby is Mettler, Weed Patch, Wheeler Ridge, Maricopa, and Santa Maria.

I gaze momentarily at Danny as he stares ahead. How he longs for a girl. If only he'd find one who would be good for him. The right girl.

Signs mark the exits to Lebec and Gorman. Crossing the wrinkled, barren hills of the Tehachapis on I-5, we merge into heavy traffic. But the traffic is heavier coming the other way from the city. Four lanes take us up into the Santa Susana Mountains to a 4,000 foot pass. The sun gone, it is twilight and cool. A flood of headlights stream along the highway across the median strip like the full, strong rivers we've seen throughout the trip. The mountains turn black; ahead is a steady wall of red taillights. The fresh coolness of the air is wonderful, but soon we must crank up the windows against the chill. A large billboard advertises Bob's Big Boy. The smog across the plain of the San Fernando Valley shrouds its lights, giving it a phantom appearance.

Once we are beyond the familiar Santa Monica Mountains and in the coastal Los Angeles plateau, I feel at home, traveling the bright, washed streets that I have come to know during many past visits. We made it, Danny and I, we made it. I choke up at the thought that tomorrow we say good-bye.

DAY FIFTEEN
Santa Monica, California

After sleeping in a familiar bed in Morris and Lil's Santa Monica apartment, I am well rested this morning. We have a relaxed breakfast of home-cooked oatmeal, bananas, hot bagels, and fresh squeezed orange juice.

"Of course, fresh squeezed", says Lil. "You're in California now."

"So I've noticed."

Phoning Jane, I tell her, "We made it. We're here at Morris and Lil's. We're both bloodied but not bowed."

"It sounds to me like you had an awful time," she replies. "Is that the way to describe two weeks with our son?"

"No," I say, feeling put down, "Danny and I are really quite happy with each other."

"That's better," she says.

Can't she appreciate the irony in my remark, that by enduring each other both Danny and I have won? By sticking it out we are more closely bound together. The bitterest enemy can become one's closest partner. Understanding another elicits appreciation and tolerance; sympathy elicits love.

Our eyes meet often as Danny and I listen to our hosts interrupt each other while telling separate stories. Soon they are talking simultaneously, each ignoring the other. Hearing only snatches of both monologues, we receive an inchoate account. The competition between them tires us.

I feel that a bond, a silent understanding, has developed between Danny and me. He is nervous about the next few days, about finding a job and a place to live.

Although he lingers with us through the morning, I am aware that he's anxious to get going. Finally at 1:30 he announces his departure. The two of us, he carrying his pack, go down the elevator in silence, and walk to the dependable pickup truck parked beneath the palms on the immaculate, flower-decked street. Standing beside the pickup, we embrace. At first I can't muster words beyond "good luck."

Before he enters the cab I add, "I'll miss you," and he seems moved. I embrace him again. "Good luck," I say again.

He needs it. And how he needs it. The right girl, the right therapist, the right summer job, the right luck.

He sits behind the steering wheel and turns on the engine while keeping the door open wide. I reach in, placing my hand on his shoulder. "Learn to love yourself," I tell him, but that's all I can say because my eyes are welling up with tears and I feel I'll be maudlin. Usually controlled in such situations, I'm startled at my emotionalism. I'm not handling this well.

As Danny drives off, I wish simply to cry; but, out there on a public street, I can't possibly give in to myself. Still, why not? Why not let it come? I must allow myself to cry for my beleaguered and unhappy son. I must.

That evening, Morris, Lil, and I join a throng of a half-million people in the park above Santa Monica Beach to watch a Fourth of July fireworks display. But neither the excitement nor the awesome rocket showers lighting up the black sky distract me from worrying about Danny. Has he found a place to stay tonight? I wonder.

Well, *I* made it in life, on the trip, didn't I? Why shouldn't he? I must believe in him more, erase my doubts.

My mind drifts among memories of innocuous incidents: the free wine in a Port Angeles restaurant, an over-weight hiker plunging along a path in Sequoia, hearing a foreign language at Moro Rock, seeking shelter against a thundershower in a doorway at the University of Chicago, the first sight of Evelyn at the entrance of Reader's Digest.

What had Danny and I accomplished? We shared two weeks of life together of our own free will. And I'm glad. Need there be more?

EPILOGUE - ONE YEAR LATER
Cape Cod, Massachusetts

Before flying back to Cape Cod, I spent the next five days in the Santa Monica library honing the journal. I have retained many sentences, unedited, exactly as I wrote them at the end of each day or in the swaying pickup while Danny drove.

Two weeks after I arrived home, Danny called to say that he found an amenable place to stay, a house, which he shares with two other men.

"Why have you waited so long to call?" I asked, frustrated that, not knowing his whereabouts, we couldn't reach him.

"I've been in bad shape," he replied.

"How so?"

"I've been too depressed to talk with anyone. I've been holed up in my room."

"All this time?"

"Yes."

"Depressed over what? Have you found a therapist?"

"Yes, a man I like."

"Is he good?"

"I think so. Anyway, I like him."

"What about a job?"

"I haven't done anything on that."

"Don't you need a job to support yourself?"

"I'm not ready, Dad."

"What do you mean 'not ready?' We had a deal; I agreed to support you only while you were in school."

"Well, I thought I might take a course…"

"Just so you won't have to work, is that it?"

"I'm not fit to work."

"I don't understand. You have a will."

"Are you saying I'm a failure?"

"Yes, you're a failure. I'm disappointed. You're doing nothing to help yourself."

Click, the dial tone sounded. Full of grief and angry confusion, I frantically called him back at the number he had given.

"I'm sorry, Danny. I care about you."

"I'm trying my best, Dad. I know it's not what you want, but I'm trying my best."

"Okay, Danny, okay."

His news was a shock. Why had he fallen apart after our trip? What happened with us to cause it? What had I done? We parted good and happy friends, never closer. Or am I deceiving myself? Had the developing conviviality and warmth of our comradeship been false after all? I was baffled.

Now, a year later, duplicating my error-strewn path, he has graduated from college with a useless degree in English. His emotions swing between depression and normalcy. Afraid to enter the adult world, having no plans to work for a second summer, he is attempting to enroll in a practical job-oriented architectural school in England by fall.

In our recent phone conversation I said, I think you'll feel better about yourself if you stop being a twenty-six year old dependent and earn your own way, at least for the summer.

"That would be a problem for me," he said.

"Are you sure you're not going on to further schooling to escape adult responsibilities?"

After a pause, he said, "I'm going to architectural

school because the degree I have isn't marketable."

"I told you that when you began. Ever hear of 'tough love?' After a while, parent birds toss their babies out of the nest. And you know, they always fly. But I suppose your mother will send you money and keep you going."

Thus Danny's emotional trouble persists. He remains dependent. He continues to see a therapist. He calls me frequently on the phone. I haven't seen him since our good-bye in Santa Monica. He tells me that he held himself back during the trip for fear of engendering my disfavor. I have urged him to offer his side of our experience for inclusion here. But he has refused.

As for my marriage, last September I separated from Jane and left our precious Cape Cod home and the garden and beach that I have loved. Ever since, her pain and mine have been beyond imagining. For a brief time a month ago we tried reconciliation, but I was unable to make it work. I left again, this time for good.

Now that I'm alone, I have more contact with my children. Our conversations are weightier, more satisfying than before. Would I do it again, another trip with Danny or with either of my daughters? You bet I would.

ADDENDUM I - TEN YEARS LATER
Mid-Coast Maine

After Danny graduated college (for which I admired him) he went off to London, England as planned, to attend an architectural school. I refused to pay his way until I had strong evidence that he was applying himself. Still, he managed to secure sufficient funds (perhaps from his mother) to maintain himself and pay tuition. After a year, finding himself ill-prepared for the required courses in science and math, he quit school and lingered in London for another year or so. During this period his infrequent letters were demanding and hostile.

Meanwhile, his mother and I, after a bitter battle over the division of our assets, were divorced. Three years later I remarried and moved to Maine, wrote five books, and found peace and happiness in my work, my marriage, and in the relaxed Maine lifestyle.

Danny returned home, met a stable, supportive girl, a social worker, married her, returned to college in Boston where he secured a masters degree in social work, and is now a practicing psychotherapist dealing mostly with troubled children from dysfunctional families. A few months ago he and his lovely wife had a perfect baby girl. They live in a home of their own in a New England seacoast town.

Needless to say, I am proud of my son. Knowing his own past troubles, of how hard life can be to some young people, he now dedicates his career to helping them. He has risen from the ashes to soar. I confess finding this remarkable. Ten years ago as we traveled across the continent, I would not have predicted such a happy outcome for either of us. He had the determination and capacity to mature and grow, and I missed seeing it.

I see now that as a man comes into his thirties, he begins to view life more calmly and realistically, takes on responsibilities and even thrives. And with the right partner by his side he's bound to succeed.

And I have also discovered that a man can start anew at any time—certainly in his sixties, no doubt later. There's no age limit. However, in my case, it was first necessary that I end a destructive relationship—although it produced three highly productive and rewarding children—and replace it with a compatible and loving one.

The human spirit, I now realize, is amazingly resilient. That premise hadn't occurred to me when Danny and I traveled together. So is the love between a father and son. Despite the misery we caused each other, Danny and I now express in many ways an abiding love. We have gratifying conversations. I enjoy being his father, and I see he enjoys being my son.

ADDENDUM II - TWENTY YEARS LATER
Mid-Coast Maine

Danny is now a mature adult of 46 years, happily married to a sensible, responsible and loving woman, and the father of two daughters, ten and five. I admire the way he and his wife are bringing up the children, setting boundaries and spending time with them together and singly. He is now well established in his community as a psychotherapist specializing in dysfunctional families as a marriage counselor and sex therapist. I suspect, since he was raised in a dysfunctional family this is no coincidence. In addition to dealing with patients he also writes an advice column in a monthly magazine regarding couples' problems. And he has a twice monthly hour long call-in radio program.

Our relationship has blossomed over the years. He seeks my advice on his investments and business matters. The other day he notified me that he was starting to build an organization of psychotherapists whom he would instruct in his specialty, thereby increasing his income and providing him with some security in case of illness or disability.

"Good thinking," I said. "You are certainly entrepreneurial. I remember when you dropped out of college to start a business building kitchens."

"Why are you surprised?" he asked. "Where do you think it comes from?"

Touché, Danny.

In fact Danny replicates the man I was at his age. He's driven to succeed, perhaps to show me what he can do. I was driven to show my mother what I could do. He does complain that he has little spare time for himself, finding bringing up the girls especially demanding. It's payback time, I remind him, but say no more. His mother and I had three children, one more than he has, with a hellion of a boy in the middle. He's got it relatively easy.

So I'm prouder than ever at what my son has become. And I am gratified at what my own life has become. I note that in the previous chapters I say nothing about my fortunes. Well, three years after our journey I married a woman a generation younger than myself. I confess at first I had a problem with our age difference, but eventually got over it as I discovered how much she and I had in common concerning our tastes and how to conduct our lives. At the time of our courtship she was a landscape artist painting Cape Cod scenes. But finding the Cape becoming crowded and excessively tourist oriented, we moved to a small coastal town in Maine where we bought and renovated a mid-18th century house.

After ten years we sold that home and moved to a summer house that we had built down a peninsula on a salt water cove in a small bucolic community. The house includes an airy, bright artist's studio for my wife and a study for myself. Having published seven books, in recent years I've been writing plays, and with my neighbors we do fund raising performance readings in our local church. Best of all, my grown children with their spouses and children visit our quiet, relaxing spot at least once a year, usually leaving each of the grandchildren behind to stay with us for a week. To celebrate my eightieth birthday the entire gang rented a cottage nearby for a week so that we could all share in being together.

When I made the cross-country trip with Danny I hadn't imagined I'd be leading such a good life in my old age. Nor did I imagine that Danny and his two sisters and I would grow much closer than we have ever been regardless of the physical distance between us. As we mature, I think, we appreciate more the sacrifices one's parents make. Even now, at my age, after almost forty years since his death I miss my father's companionship. How will Danny and his sisters think of me once I'm gone? Today, from all indications, it will be favorable. I could wish for nothing more.